TMI

(Truthful Marriage Insights)

MADISON PENNER

 FriesenPress

Suite 300 - 990 Fort St
Victoria, BC, V8V 3K2
Canada

www.friesenpress.com

ISBN
978-1-5255-6144-3 (Hardcover)
978-1-5255-6145-0 (Paperback)
978-1-5255-6146-7 (eBook)

1. FAMILY & RELATIONSHIPS, MARRIAGE

Distributed to the trade by The Ingram Book Company

Contents

Prelude:

Hi there!

Welcome to my inner thoughts regarding marriage. I am Madison, a twenty-three-year-old wife and home keeper living in the middle of farming country in Manitoba, Canada. I and my wonderful husband, Ryan, have been married for almost a year and half and, although it has had its challenges, it has also been the best thing I've ever experienced. I am an outspoken, honest, tell-it-like-it-is kind of gal who has a mission to see marriages (especially my own) be all that they can be. This book is something I have been thinking about for a long time, and it has finally made its way from my head out onto the pages you are now holding. Though I don't pretend to think that we have it all together, I do think that personal, honest testimony about the early stages of marriage can be eye opening and helpful if that is what you are about to embark on, or if you are experiencing it yourself. As the title suggests, this book is going to get into the un-pretty, hilariously honest, and unashamedly open realities about what early marriage was like for my husband and me. My hope and desire would be that God could use some of what we learned to give you encouragement, make you feel like you have a friend, and strengthen you when you feel like you just can't get it all together.

Acknowledgements

My sweet husband, Ryan, you have taught me what true Christ-like love is. You work so hard every day to make this marriage incredible. Thank you for your support, your encouragement, and your constant belief that I can achieve whatever I set my mind to.

Chapter 1:
Wedding Day Jitters

I sat perched on the edge of a chair in my family's large kitchen, hair wand high above my head with my long hair twizzled around it. Around me there was excited chattering, laughing, hubbub, and commotion as the flurry of activity that was my wedding morning ensued. Away from all that, I was somewhere in my mind contemplating what the day was about to bring, the commitment I was about to make, and the gravity of this heavy thing called "marriage."

Marriage wasn't something that I've taken lightly . . . ever. You will understand that this makes perfect sense when you consider that my parents were separated from the time I was born until I was seven years old. Although they did re-marry each other after their long separation, the (second) honeymoon phase eventually passed, and my older brother and I were once again thrown into the daily chaos of an off-kilter marriage, this time in the company of two newly added younger siblings. In the years leading up to my meeting my soon-to-be husband, the environment of my family home had dissolved into poorly veiled fights, watery eyes, threats to leave, and uncomfortable tension. Though they promised to never separate again, the confidence we kids had in that promise was slipping more with every day that passed.

In the midst of the peak of this uncertainty at home, I met my darling man, Ryan, at an annual church conference in the middle of the Saskatchewan prairies. I came every year from my hometown of Fort McMurray, Alberta, and he came every year from his hometown of Portage la Prairie, Manitoba. It was there, smack dab in the middle, that we began what, five months later, would be him down on one knee asking me to marry him.

As I curled my hair and stared into my eyes in the mirror on the morning of our wedding three months after our engagement, I faced a frightening question: *Could I do a better job of being married?* I mentally ticked off the advantages I hoped our marriage would have. *One, the Lord had showed each of us through prayer and scripture that we were the ones He had chosen for each other. Two, we had been extremely careful to maintain purity before marriage and had started doing preparation marriage counselling before we were even engaged. Three, we both had established convictions about our doctrinal beliefs coming into our relationship. And, four, Ryan was good to me. I could always love a man who was so diligent at caring for me and making me feel like his special princess. Couldn't I?* At that moment though, staring down the belief that I could be genetically mutated to suck at marriage, all of those "advantages" felt like they could mean nothing at all.

Despite the fears I had and my uncertainty about what lay before me, I was up at the front of the church by about 11 a.m., bouquet trembling, stomach churning, pledging my life to the man before me. As I said the words we had written as vows some weeks earlier, I felt the weight of what I was promising to Ryan.

"I, Madison, do take you, Ryan, to be my husband. I give myself to you in marriage from this day forward, to love, honour, and cherish you through every circumstance we may encounter. With the Lord's help, I will learn to follow your leadership and show you a constant Christ-like love. Therefore, no matter what lies ahead, I pledge my life to you as a loving and faithful wife."

I didn't expect to feel so scared on my wedding day. I didn't expect to look at Ryan and see that same fear. Did it mean that we were somehow failing? Did it mean that we weren't as in love as other couples or that we wouldn't make it through? All I could think in the moment was: *This is it. You are actually vowing your whole life to another person. This. Is. It.*

~

Thankfully, that *was* it! That was the day that I married the man whom God had prepared for me and who is now my best friend. Looking back, I can still remember all of the fear and the scary uncertainty of what was to come. I was struggling to fully trust in God and put my expectations for not only the day but my whole future in His hands. I couldn't seem to grasp the restful peace of knowing that He had chosen Ryan for me and that we had been brought together for a reason. Despite the fact that my soul was quaking, thankfully, with a whole lot a prayer and a little faith, I got to start my life with my husband that day.

My intention in telling you my inner thoughts on our wedding day is not to scare you, and definitely not to make you doubt. My intention is to speak to those who are preparing for their wedding day and have experienced these feelings and to tell them that it is OK to be afraid and to have conflicting emotions. I went into our wedding day having no idea that I might not feel like I was on cloud nine. I had no idea that all of the sudden it would hit me that I was making a choice for the rest of my life and that I'd be shaking in my boots. For a while after the wedding I thought that there was something wrong with me. I was afraid that my own response to my wedding day was self-fulfilling prophesy that we wouldn't be able to have a good marriage or that I would fail as a wife.

From this side of marriage I am very thankful to say that it's OK if you don't get "cloud-nine" feelings. There's nothing wrong with you and, with the Lord's help, anyone can have a good marriage. I had to realize a few things before I was able to let go of my fears and fully rely on God for the success and happiness of our marriage. My desire is to share those things in this chapter, with the hope that you can be encouraged and prepared for whatever lies ahead, stomach in knots or not.

T-R-U-S-T. Trust in G-O-D

When I considered Ryan as a potential husband I knew that I couldn't just trust my own gut. The conference weekend we met, we both did a lot of praying and a lot of searching. Now I know that exchanging numbers is a far cry from actually saying "I do," but to both of us it was very important that we didn't start a relationship if we didn't feel like the Lord was leading us into it. We didn't know this until much later in our relationship, but by the time Ryan came across the church parking lot to talk to me (paper and pen in his pocket), we had both separately communicated with the Lord and reached the peaceful conclusion that exchanging numbers was what He had in mind for us to do next.

This peace was something we both relied on many a day during our long-distance relationship and it was the main thing that I was relying on when I was up at the altar, shaking in my boots and committing my life to a man I'd only known for eight months. In that moment I could look back to the day everything had started for us and say for certain that God had led us together and that my marrying Ryan was His plan for my life.

If you are heading into marriage I want you to know that it is absolutely crucial that you know if the person you are in a relationship with is who God wants for you. I have seen through my life that a God-given assurance about who you are marrying can bring so much confidence and peace even during the hardest struggles of marriage. This is amazing because not one of us is perfect. Even though I adore my Ryan, and even though he makes me believe that angels really do walk among us, sometimes I still struggle to trust him. Even in the midst of our beautiful lives we sometimes both doubt our ability to have a successful marriage. At these times both of us can rest in the confidence of God's plan for us and know for certain that He not only designed marriage but that He matched us for marriage. When we struggle to trust each other or ourselves we can put all our trust in God.

Great Expectations

I know that as little girls we plan out the perfect wedding and imagine just how fulfilling that moment of entering through the double doors will be. We watch romantic movies with our hearts fluttering at the thought of a man looking at us the way Darcy looks at Elizabeth in the morning mist. In our daydreams, the first kiss often includes the angel chorus ringing out "Hallelujah!" and a cinematic fanfare as your groom dips you gently and leans in for a passionate kiss.

All of these things are great and amazing, but what happens if you don't feel any of the proverbial butterflies? What happens if your groom is just as scared as you are and instead of a soft, longing look of passion you see a hint of fear? What happens if not every memory of your wedding day is something you want to revisit?

Before you freak out like I did and wonder if you even love your groom if your bouquet shakes in your hand all the way up the aisle or if your wedding was a failure because it didn't feel like "the best day of your life," let me stop you there and give you a virtual hug and tell you it's going to be OK.

First of all, your wedding day isn't the day to expect to feel every little heart flutter or butterfly. As a nurse, I can truthfully tell you that when your heart rate is already hitting close to a hundred, you are very unlikely to feel an extra little flop when you see your groom for the first time. Also when your stomach is in knots, the butterflies don't have any room to fly (a fact that is not exactly scientific, but still quite accurate).

Secondly, when you get to the front of the aisle and look into your groom's eyes, know that the look you should expect is less of a Matthew McConaughey smolder and more of an "On the count of three we will jump from the aircraft. Make sure to pull your chute." Not that your groom isn't committed or excited to marry you, but he is likely just as scared as you are.

Lastly—and I feel, most importantly—every moment on your wedding day may not be the movie reel you were expecting, but that is *all right*. I married a man who lived 1,555 kilometres away from my hometown and family. My wedding day was not only the day I would be married, but the last day I was ever going to call my family home, home. This situation made for a roller coaster of emotions as the day progressed.

I remember one moment in particular that was especially difficult for me to revisit after my wedding day. I was in the bathroom following the reception. My husband was waiting outside to take me away to our hotel, but I had whisked my mom in there with me to help hold my dress's endless layers of tulle skirt while I took care of things. The typical laughter at the awkwardness of the situation took place, but as I was fixing my hair in the mirror afterward, my mom just looked at me and started crying. We both knew that this moment was one of the last we would have together before I moved two provinces away to start my new life. In the three months of my engagement to Ryan I had packed up my life in a seemingly emotionless state. I hadn't once allowed myself to cry, and had staunchly refused to acknowledge that there was grief involved with giving up one life for another. But in that moment, I looked at the face of the woman who had cared for me for the last twenty-one years and felt like I had failed her. Felt like I hadn't spent enough time, felt like I should have cried with her before, and felt a reluctance to let go that made letting go so much harder.

In that moment, I felt real, hard sadness, which came crashing into feelings of anxiety, joy, excitement, and fear, mixing up the strangest tasting cocktail my heart had ever been served. When I looked back, I would try to separate out the feelings that weren't what I expected as the "typical" wedding day excitement and would only want to re-live the good feelings. What I discovered though was that this kind of feeling control isn't possible, and I was confronted with either changing my expectations of the day or throwing the proverbial baby out with the bathwater.

I want you to know that feeling a range of emotions on your wedding day is OK! Good ones, bad ones, neutral ones—you may feel them all, but don't worry, God's got you! He is right there by your side, He led you here, and He will lead you still. From this side of my wedding day, I can look back and see it for everything it was, both happy and hard. But what is most special is that I can see how my relationship with God grew through the experience of fully trusting Him with my future. Oddly enough, the very verse that God used to confirm His approval of Ryan seeking a relationship with me was the verse I needed to help me manage my expectations. In Jeremiah 29:11, it says, "For I know the thoughts that I think towards you, saith the Lord, thoughts of *peace*, and not of evil, to give you and *expected* end" (KJV). When the Lord says "expected end" in this verse, He is referring to our future. The future that He planned for us when He made us! For me, this future included a dark and handsome, brown-eyed man that I vowed my life to on a beautiful day in December. That day I needed to put my expectations in the hands of my Creator and trust Him to see me through the vast array of my emotions and the fear that was trying to break in. I needed to understand that what felt like emotional failure was actually triumph because, despite the fear, despite the uncertainty, on a beautiful day in December I married the best guy God could have ever given me.

Conclusion

I hope that on your wedding day you will be able to set your expectations in God's capable hands. I hope that you can fully trust and rely on Him to help you through the day and future with your spouse. I hope that you will look back and treasure all of the little moments of your day, no matter where they lie on the emotional spectrum. Most of all, I hope that even if you shake the flowers off your bouquet on your way down the aisle that you can stand there and, with confidence, proclaim to love, honour, and cherish a man that you know God has brought into your life to be your husband.

Chapter 2: Intimacy

My car pulled to a stop in front of my friend's house just as the front door was swinging open. Through my passenger window I could see my fiancé emerge from the doorway and onto the small landing at the top of the steep staircase that led down to the sidewalk. I smiled, pulled on my door handle, stepped out of my vehicle, and turned back to the house just in time to hear Ryan let out a little grunt as his feet slipped out from under him and he went thumping down all eight of the wooden stairs. I hurried around the car and tried to help him to his feet, but the grimace on his face and the way he was holding his arm didn't bode very well.

About an hour later we were sitting in the Fort McMurray emergency room, both looking rather deflated. We learned that he had a hairline fracture to the ulna bone in his right arm. Soon after, a nurse came in, applied a half cast, placed his arm in a sling, gave him some Tylenol, and sent us on our way. Rather than head to my parents' home to rest on the couch or take some time off to recover from a broken arm, we both packed up and headed to the church to decorate. Why, you may ask, would we do a loony thing like that? Well, because we were set to get married in three days.

Now I know I might have mentioned that I love Ryan, but have I mentioned that I LOVE Ryan?! Broken arm, face white with pain, and yet he was still in the ceremony space lining up chairs with the laser guide that my dad (who has a touch of undiagnosed OCD) had brought to get the rows "just right." He worked tirelessly to make sure the space was beautiful for our big day, listening to my stress as I (who inherited that touch of undiagnosed OCD) lined up all of the cutlery on the tables for our reception. By the end of the day we both fell, exhausted, into my parents' couch and sat quietly, one major thing rolling around in both of our minds: *How the heck are we going to make love in three days?*

~

Now listen, I know that this book is titled *TMI*, but even *I* know that you don't share the details of intimacy in marriage unless it is with your mom. So without getting in depth on it, suffice to say that where there is a will, there is a way, and our wedding night and honeymoon turned out just fine. Sure, Ryan took a little more Tylenol than may have been necessary if he was just doing the Netflix part of "Netflix and chill," but he lived. All joking aside though, despite a beautiful honeymoon and an incredible wedding night, we came to our new home in Manitoba and felt like somehow we weren't enjoying intimacy like we should be.

Ryan and I had committed to not kissing each other on the mouth before we got married. So our very first kiss was up on the stage in front of everyone after our officiate announced, "You may now kiss the bride." The multiple kisses that we had at the reception after that were all good, but we weren't practiced at all, so I came away convinced that our guests felt somewhat like Tony Stark's friend in *Iron Man 2* when he says they looked like "two seals fighting over a grape."

Whether that was true, our decision to not kiss before our wedding meant that everything about a physical relationship between us was new. I found myself stressing after the wedding because I didn't feel those elusive butterflies when we kissed. I didn't just imagine my husband naked and get turned on. I didn't feel comfortable with the lights on or particularly like being seen. I couldn't enjoy my own body's reaction to lovemaking if I didn't purposely focus on it. I didn't feel all of these "things" I thought I was supposed to feel!

During that time (about three months), I was looking for anything to read that could tell me that I was normal. Anything that could confirm that even if I wasn't fifty years old and going through menopause I could still have some difficulties enjoying a physical relationship. Unfortunately, I couldn't find anything that spoke to the newlywed Christian girl who had kept her virginity for marriage. So I pressed on, I prayed, I talked to God about the nitty-gritty of my feelings, and we made it through to a love life in our marriage that is more fulfilling everyday. What I learned through that time though, are some things that I want to share with you in the rest of this chapter.

It takes time to make a thing go right

Full disclosure, for our wedding night I booked a hotel that had a Jacuzzi so that I could get comfortable with the notion of being naked around my husband in the "land of strategically placed bubbles." While this strategy only worked so-so, it did make me realize that it was going to take some time before I felt comfortable with my body belonging to someone else. The best part, though, is that it's OK if it takes some time to adjust. When you keep a tight lid on your virginity it means that when you do finally open it up and let it out, it is going to take some time before it is comfortable in the outside world. Now, if you are thinking that this makes keeping your virginity only for your husband a disadvantage, you are so very mistaken. One of the most beautiful things I have discovered is that God knows what He is doing when He tells us, "Do not stir up or awaken love before it pleases" (Song of Sol. 2:7, KJV). These things are hard to describe and are meant to be discovered by a couple by themselves, but let me just say that learning about intimate love together is one of the most precious things you can give to each other in marriage. When you choose to save this gift for each other, however, it is important to know that it will take time in marriage before a physical relationship is (a) second nature, and (b) easily enjoyable.

If kissing is something you choose to save for marriage and it doesn't feel like electricity every time your lips touch, don't panic. Keep at it! Kiss often, don't over-think it, just lean in, eyes closed, and do whatever feels right. In time, you will likely get better at it, and in time your brain will just relax and enjoy the thrill of making out with your handsome hubby. Don't be like me and have a total crisis because you are afraid that you will never enjoy kissing your husband. You will! Just give it some time.

OK, now I'm praying that you have chosen to save intimacy for marriage, because it is super important and amazing to be able to give this gift just to your spouse. When you have saved it, it can be daunting to think about before you get married. Society around us can sometimes make us feel like we really need to know what we are doing before we get to the bedroom. At the same time, looking stuff like this up can be really harmful to keeping your thoughts pure before you get married. What I would like to encourage you to do is just stop and pray. Ryan used to tell me that Adam and Eve had never googled sex and they did just fine. In the same way, God would give each of us wisdom and some instinct when it came time to be intimate with each other (he was right, of course). By communicating with God rather than Google, it is easier to put your fears and insecurities down and just enjoy the beauty of what God designed marital intimacy to be.

That all being said, a comfort with real-life, naked intimacy will likely take some time to develop. In the beginning I would encourage you to adjust things to make it as comfortable as it can be. For example, if you are a bit insecure like I was, turn down the lights and light a candle (turns out this is not just mood setting, but flattering lighting). If you would rather cuddle under the sheets, suggest that to your spouse until you are secure enough to be openly admired in just your skin. Most importantly, don't give up on it! God has placed all sorts of delights into love-making that are just waiting to be explored by couples. If you push through the phase of awkwardness you will discover that intimacy just gets better and better!

I want you to want me

One of the biggest reasons it's so important to keep making love, even through the awkward phase, is because your hubby really needs it. Now wait just a minute before your inner feminist starts climbing onto her soap box and proclaiming how men's needs shouldn't rule the world. I understand that response because that was my immediate reaction, once upon a time. I used to think that it was ridiculous for men to act like they needed sex or that somehow their needs were greater than a woman's. Then I got married, and understood something pretty crazy about a guy's needs. A guy just needs to be needed.

So, listen, I don't have the time it would take to get into how men need to be aware that there are times when a woman doesn't feel like having intercourse. Or how, obviously, guilting your wife into having sex or pushing your needs onto her to get your way is wrong. For this book I am mainly talking to the ladies, so, gals, here's a secret. God has created a way for you to show your husband that you need and desire everything about him. That is through sex.

When you indicate to your husband that you want to make love with him and when you go to your marriage bed wholeheartedly with passionate abandon, he feels like he is on top of the world. If you reluctantly agree to make love and allow him to have the release his body is craving without actually making *him* feel needed, it is like giving him his favourite desert but poisoning it at the same time. I have learned through marriage that men don't just crave the physical release of sex, but they crave the emotional fulfillment it gives them. After a hard day or a difficult discussion we women may feel better after a long cry and a hug, but lovemaking, to them, is a hug to their soul that re-assures them that they are still needed and wanted. Rather than withholding this kind of love from our husbands, we women really need to learn to be selfless lovers who use sex as a tool to express our deep longing for our man. There will be times when we truly can't make love, and I will address ways to communicate that at the end of this chapter, but for now, just know that the attitude with which we approach sex can be the difference between it being an act of love and an act of physical release.

When it comes to the actual physical release part of lovemaking, there are a lot of mechanics involved in the process that make it a skill to be learned rather than a talent you are born with. Let's just say that at the beginning of marriage my husband and I lay down on our bed one day and had a good laugh about how movies often hint at multiple encounters during one night (yeah, right). Though we have learned a lot since then, we still say we would rather take quality over quantity and we are sticking to that motto.

The quality of lovemaking is directly related to your communication, which I will talk about in a minute, and also to how you learn and adjust from sexual experience. The way we view intimacy isn't the only difference between girls and boys in the bedroom. For the most part, girls take a much longer time to reach a climax than a guy. Does this mean then that you shouldn't bother trying to climax together? No! This just means that the two of you will likely need to figure out how to get your timing closer together. Now, I'm not about to get into how to do that because I'm only me, and you are you, and I don't get paid enough to delve that deep on this. All I'm saying is that timing a climax together *is* possible and you should absolutely keep trying to find ways to make love better and better.

If you are wondering why I keep stressing working on lovemaking and getting better at it, it is because I honestly believe that lovemaking should be a regular habit in your marriage. Yup, I said it. Lovemaking should be as natural to your marriage as watching a TV show before bed is. Once again, I get it, there are definitely times where our bodies are resetting their cycle or where you are both just too tired and that is OK. But I believe that God created sex to connect a husband and a wife in a way that nothing else can. I don't have children yet, so I cannot speak to the love life of a mom, but as a young married woman, I think that making love should be a multiple-times-per-week kind of thing. Now, hear me out before this gets too overwhelming. God says in the Bible that, "The two shall become one flesh" (Mark 10:8, KJV). When you and your husband are intimate, you, for a short time, physically become joined as one person. You can be as good at communicating as you want to, and always be "on the same page," but nothing else will replicate the feeling of being one like making love will. I'm not going to say exactly how frequent this needs to be for you, but I do believe that sex needs to be treated as though it is a tool as important as good communication. Without utilizing all of the tools in your marriage toolbox, you may have difficulty feeling connected as a couple or being as closely "one" as God created us to be.

Express yourself

As promised, I am going to pull communication out of the marriage toolbox and seek to address all of the special knobs and buttons this little gadget has to help us in the bedroom. Without communication regarding sex, we will run into a bunch of problems. First: not knowing how to bring our spouse pleasure or not telling them how to do that for us. Second: constantly wondering if lovemaking is "to be or not to be" for the duration of the evening then having it sprung on you at the last minute. Third: running into troubles with your love life and having no way to problem-solve them. In the following pages, I hope to discuss some of the things we found helpful in our first year and inspire you to find new ways to communicate about sex in your marriage.

The first thing I learned about lovemaking was on our wedding night. Now, before you ball up into one big sphere of cringe, I am not going to go too in-depth on this because, obviously, we two virgins learned a lot on our wedding night. But what I learned that I'd like to share with you is that it's necessary to do what Charles Wright sings in one of his hit songs and "express yourself!" Your hubby won't know what to do for you unless you tell him, and you won't know what to do for him unless he tells you. The more open and honest you can be with each other, the better. Now, don't stress. It takes some time to get good at expressing yourself to your spouse, but it is much like intimacy and should be practised.

I was shocked when I discovered that lots of couples, even ones married for a long time, communicate through their whole marriage then get into the bedroom and become mute. Though it sometimes gets me into trouble, I have never been one to hold back what I was thinking. In fact, Ryan and I discovered through our pre-marriage counselling that I typically think things through outside of my head, meaning I actually need to *verbalize* my thoughts to process them. Thankfully, this equates to my never struggling to communicate with Ryan in the bedroom. If you are the kind though that processes inside your head and finds it really hard to let out your feelings it is OK! With dedicated practice and time you will be able to share what you need with your husband. What is most important though is realizing the value of this and really working on implementing transparent communication during lovemaking with your man.

The second thing I learned about intimacy, when I was settled into normal married life, was that the only thing on my mind after supper was washing the dishes. Granted, that could be my undiagnosed OCD acting up, but truthfully, without intentional thought and planning on my part, by the time Ryan got home I was about as turned on as a potato. So I did some searching, some of the soul and some of the internet, and discovered that I needed to think about making love during the day if I wanted to want it by nighttime. Seems simple enough, eh? Well, at first it wasn't, but I got better at it. I'd be washing dishes and try to think about all sorts of sexy things, but what I found was that it took some practice before this strategy really took root. After some time though, I became better at setting my intention to make love and truly desiring it by the time Ryan returned from work.

One thing in particular that helped me set my intention was stating it. Like actually texting Ryan and saying, "Honey, I can't wait until you are home tonight and we can make love." Or sending him a sexy picture of me and telling him that I was looking forward to showing him more of me later. This did two things for us. First of all, it helped Ryan to know what he could expect when he came home. Second, it helped me to stay in the mindset of wanting to make love because I was talking about it with him and had told him my intentions, which I would aim to never go back on.

It is very important that you keep your word after you have stated your intentions regarding intimacy. I know that circumstances can change, and I am not saying that Ryan or I have never changed our minds about making love, but for the most part, we make it a policy to discuss our desires and stick to them. If you promise intimacy and get your husband all excited and then you turn him down, he can feel very unwanted and this kind of thing can eventually break trust.

One thing I would like to talk about for a moment is how to lovingly turn down your husband's request for intimacy. I went through a phase around the one-year mark of our marriage when I rarely wanted to make love. The birth control pills I was on were really messing with my libido and it felt like any time we were intimate I had to put in so much effort to show enthusiasm and delight. The sex was great, I loved my man, but I just couldn't get my body to show up for the party. During this time there were lots of nights when I turned down intimacy because I just couldn't get turned on. Now, a huge part of this being OK was Ryan's understanding and loving response to my needs, but it would take a whole other book written by a man to address how to respond like this. For now, I'm just addressing what we women can do in this situation and what has worked for me. The most successful way I have found to decline sex is to reassure your husband that you want him, but tell him the reasons your body isn't up to it. Once again, if he feels unwanted he will feel hurt—it is so important to make sure he knows he is desired even if you cannot use your body to show it.

The last thing I want to share that I learned about intimacy is perhaps the one that I found most surprising. That would be that lovemaking is a God thing. Meaning that God not only designed it for us, but that He is interested in helping us get as much pleasure from it as possible. This may sound odd, but I couldn't tell you how many times Ryan has held me close, nothing between us but skin, face burrowed in my hair, and started praying to God to help us bring enjoyment and fulfillment to each other during our intimate time together. At first this seemed like a bit of an odd thing to me, but pretty quickly I realized how incredible it is that we can bring this to God. Nothing about sex in marriage is dirty or wrong. Nothing about sex in marriage is displeasing to God. We can honestly approach Him and ask Him to help us when we are having a hard time getting turned on. We can ask Him to clear our minds during bedroom time with our spouse. We can even ask Him to help us think of new and honouring ways to fulfill our husband's needs. Once you have brought God into the bedroom like that you won't be able to help but thank Him when He shows you the fullness of the incredible act of love that is sex!

Conclusion

Ryan and I are still learning new and amazing things about this facet of our marriage everyday, but these few things I have shared have sure helped us through the beginning phases. I hope through this chapter you have understood that it is OK to not be an expert the first day on the job. I hope that you have found help and encouragement in what I have learned about intimacy with my husband. Most of all, I hope that you keep trying to make love better and that you bring God into the bedroom with you as you build and enhance your intimate relationship with your husband.

Chapter 3: Communication

I love Ryan, and I am his wife now. I am supposed to want to live here. This mantra played over and over in my head as the day stretched on and the permanence of my situation pressed down on my overwhelmed heart. It was two weeks after our wedding day, and one week after I had moved to rural Manitoba. I had been unpacking all day, slowly finding places to store my belongings in our new house. With each item I unpacked it seemed like my old life was slipping away, inch by inch, and I was desperate to stop it.

By the time evening fell I was emotionally and physically exhausted. Ryan (husband extraordinaire that he is) coaxed me into bed, wrapped me in his arms, and let me cry into his chest. I was terrified. Every doubt I had had about marriage was coming true. I couldn't be committed, I couldn't love enough. I didn't even want to live here and I had only been *here* for one week! All of my greatest fears reared their heads and stared me down with unrelenting intimidation. I wished I could just return everything back to normal and resume the life I was used to. Overwhelmed and upset, tears streaming down my face, I turned to Ryan and spoke some of the hardest words he has ever heard.

"I want to go home."

I saw his eyes widen and the air hung between us as I realized that I had actually voiced the terrible thought I had been thinking all day. I stiffened, waiting for him to release his hold on me and leave our room. I had pushed him too far. No man would be able to take the betrayal those words held and still want to hold the woman that said them. No man would hear those things from their new bride and still try to communicate with her. What had I done?

I could feel his heart beating faster as the impact of my words hit him. A few seconds ticked by, but rather than feel his arms slip away I felt them tighten as he pressed a kiss to the top of my head and swallowed around the lump in his throat. His voice was thick with emotion as he spoke the words that I will never forget.

"If you go home I will just follow you there."

My heart stopped as the meaning of what he was saying sunk in. I had expected him to exasperatedly ask me what more I could want from him, or to growl that I was an impossible woman to live with. I had been waiting for him to storm out of our room and slam the door of the house, or to maybe yell at me that I *should* go home. What I had not expected, however, was for him to listen to my hurtful words, take them all into his gentle heart, and communicate love back to me in the purest form I had ever seen. It was such a foreign response to me that I lay stunned in his arms for a few moments as I absorbed how much he loved me. What his words had communicated was more than a commitment to follow me. They had also said to me that he truly, whole-heartedly, Prince-Charming-style, loved me!

I had never known a love like that, never seen it in my home, and maybe never even believed it existed. The kind of love that would pursue you and hold you and consistently care for you was something I thought was just a Bible story. In that moment though, I discovered that Christ-like love was real, not just an unattainable standard. Though what I'd said had hurt him, through his words Ryan was able to not only calm my fears but reassure me that he truly loved me. This instance, along with many others in our early marriage, helped me to realize the important part that communication plays in a marriage and how it can enhance our love for one another.

The topic of communication may seem overwhelming, and heaven knows that I struggled to even communicate in this book about what I have learned. But take heart! God *wants* to see good communication in marriages and He will always be alongside to help. There was never a moment when we couldn't both bow our heads and seek God during a hard conversation, and never a time when He didn't answer with the guidance that we needed. What I want to discuss in this chapter was challenging to learn and hard to experience, but incredibly rewarding to see grow. I hope the things I share will encourage you to press on, and will help to enhance your communication as you tackle the challenges that early marriage brings.

Help me to help you

When Ryan and I were first married, I didn't find it very hard to share how I felt about things. Good things, bad things, and everything in between. I would crawl in bed with him, lay my head on his chest, talk about my feelings, then— bam—tears everywhere. For him, however, sharing feelings wasn't so easy, and there were lots of things that we both had to learn to improve this area of our communication. First off, it was actually hard for him to share feelings when I offloaded so many emotions onto him. Second, men in general are used to sharing facts with one another, so it was often hard for him to identify what he felt versus what were facts. Lastly, I would want Ryan to share his feelings, but became scared and emotional when he told me what was going on inside of his heart. This often inspired the opposite result to what I was seeking, and caused him to actually withhold his feelings in an attempt to shelter me. If this is something you are going through currently, fear not! Through many long conversations and lots of trial and error, we have learned that there are definitely some things that can be done to help each other share feelings, and to improve our understanding of each other.

As I mentioned in the first chapter, there was a lot of unrest and dysfunction in my family's home when I started dating Ryan. My parents' tumultuous marriage caused me a lot of fears, which meant I brought a lot of proverbial baggage to our relationship. Ryan, sweet soul that he is, gently and lovingly helped me unpack this baggage through the first year of our marriage. While I couldn't thank him enough for helping me deal with my past and loving me through every fear, I didn't realize until much later that I was monopolizing the emotional care in our marriage. During the first year, I opened up and shared every fear and hurt I had accumulated over the twenty-two years of life I had lived. Meanwhile, he was trying his very best to be my support and protector, but some of my fears where scaring him, too. By the time I realized this, my poor hubby had a lot of feelings and fears that I hadn't realized were there and hadn't taken the time to love away.

While we may feel like men are tough and strong and have no hurts or emotions under that chiselled exterior, it turns out they are actually almost as human as the rest of us. God has given them this amazing desire though to be our knights in shining armour and to protect us. So as long as we are the ones needing love and emotional care, they will be tough and strong and keep the feelings they are accumulating to themselves. This is so heroic and sweet of them, but I learned that it can be really hard on your knight to hide the wounds he has under his armour just so he can carry you through the fire. Am I saying that I couldn't rely on my husband to care for my emotional needs? No! He still always wants to be needed! What I am saying though, is that it was super important to take the time to take care for him and find out *his* emotional needs.

How exactly do you find out a man's emotional needs? You ask him! Now wait, before you look at me like I have four heads, yes, I know men don't often sit down and have big ol' heart to hearts. This kind of emotional reveal takes some practice on his part, and a whole lot of listening and loving on yours. What I did find was when I started to ask my husband what he felt, he responded with the facts of the situation rather than actual emotions. This was different, but great! I actually called it progress because, believe it or not, I learned that facts were my hubby "mansplaining" his feelings. Ryan is typically very logical, so without practice, his emotions mostly came out sounding like he was listing the facts of the day. With time though, he learned to identify what he was feeling in a given moment and to share that with me.

One practice we implemented in our marriage to help enhance this was for Ryan to share one feeling every day. In the beginning this was very general, such as him expressing that he felt frustrated because he didn't get as much work done as he was hoping to, or that he was happy because it was nice weather. At first, even this wasn't entirely comfortable for Ryan to express, but with time, he started sharing feelings before I even asked for them. This was a stepping stone to his learning how to communicate even deeper feelings and to my learning how to listen to him.

We quickly learned that asking about feelings regarding work is one thing, but asking about feelings regarding deeper subjects was a whole different ball game. This was a time when I had to do a whole lot of growing. How Ryan felt about situations or people at work didn't affect me, but how he felt about our future plans did. I could listen to his work drama and none of it ever really caused fears or feelings in me. But once Ryan got really good at sharing we started to dive into how he felt about things like having babies and raising children. This. Was. Scary. When he was sharing a feeling he had about something that directly impacted my future (such as babies), I would often come away with a whole lot of feelings, too. We had a bit of a rocky patch during this time when he would regret sharing his heart with me because he could see how it caused me fears. It took some practice on my part before I got good at listening and being supportive even when what he was saying gave me feelings, too. When he had the courage to share the burdens of his heart with me, and to trust me to take some of the load, I had to remember that this was a time to take care of his emotional needs, not mine. While this didn't come right away, we continued to work on it, and have reached a stage in our communication journey at which we can both share our feelings safely with each other.

With time and work, Ryan and I have been able to develop a way of communicating that meets both of our emotional needs. If this is something you and your husband are still working on, don't give up! Often our conversations would span a couple of hours before we had addressed and sorted out each other's feelings. The more we practiced though, the shorter this time became, and the sooner we were able to help each other overcome fears. Through God's help and guidance, we have been able to learn how to communicate more effectively with one another and as a result have grown closer. This may be difficult at the start, but keep pressing on! It is completely worth it in the end. With time and growth it is entirely possible to develop communication that can take care of both your emotional needs at the same time. If this doesn't come right away, don't panic! The important thing is that you continue to be open to listen to the feelings your husband has, and that you show care for his heart. If you learn to listen to and love away your husband's fears, you will be able to develop a closer and more open relationship.

Speak love to me

Oh, snap! I've learned the magic code!

Have you read Gary Chapman's book, *The 5 Love Languages*? If you have then you will understand why those were my exact thoughts when I learned what Ryan's love language was. If you haven't then I would definitely recommend it to you!

The basic premise of the book is that there are five languages with which people speak or understand love. The different "dialects" of love are quality time, physical touch, acts of service, words of affirmation, and gifts. Chapman does a way better job of explaining the idea, but basically everybody understands love in one of those five ways. So, for example, I am a person who feels loved if you spend quality time with me. Not that I can't feel loved other ways, but if Ryan did all sorts of nice things for me without spending time with me, I would end up feeling unloved. Ryan, on the other hand, is the type of guy who just lights up when you give him a sincere compliment. By affirming who he is with my words, I can really help him to feel loved. Seems easy enough, eh? Well,

I suppose it should be, but in the beginning, we both had a lot of learning before this became natural to us.

When I first discovered that Ryan needed words to feel loved I thought that learning his love language would be a cinch. I soon realized, though, that I was underestimating the work it would take to become fluent at speaking love to him. Growing up at home, we were often very sarcastic and jokey with one another, and I do not recall specifically affirming many people with my words. I wanted so desperately to speak love to Ryan, but I wasn't comfortable or good at affirming him in the beginning. It took dedicated practice on my part as I stumbled through awkward compliments and forced-sounding praise. Because it was something I had rarely spoken, I stammered like someone learning a second language. Thankfully, with time, I was slowly able to get more comfortable with verbally affirming my husband and was able to develop my skills at speaking love to him. Similarly, it took a while before Ryan learned to speak love to me through spending time. He discovered that I loved discussing my day with him in the evening and that I felt super special if he planned a date for us. Now, this kind of thing takes time to learn. Just like you wouldn't expect to learn Spanish in a month, you shouldn't expect to become fluent in speaking a different love language overnight. The important thing that I would encourage you to do is to keep trying!

If you are like me, your first compliment might come out sounding like, "Hey, nice face you have there." But with continued effort, you *will* be able to learn a new love language. In the beginning, I would despair of ever effectively fulfilling Ryan's needs, and there were days when he, too, wondered how he could make me feel loved. Something that has really reassured me along the way is Philippians 1:6: "He who began a good work in you will carry it on to completion"(KJV). God, who created both of you, who brought you together and who has been with you every step of the way, will be your help and guide. There may be times when you, like me, feel helplessly inadequate to show love to your partner, but in those times you can ask God to show you ways to love each other and He *will* help.

Another thing Ryan and I have learned to do when we are coming up short on how to communicate love is just to ask each other. I know what you are thinking: *Communicate about how to communicate? Crazy!* Sometimes, though, we make things so complicated when we could just ask the other person what would be special to them. Since I do not understand love through being affirmed, I often don't know what would mean the most to Ryan. In those situations, I have learned that the best thing I can do is ask him what means the most. I have often been surprised by his answer, and it has re-affirmed my decision to get his input. For example, he just loves a simple "Thank you" after he has done something for me. Similarly, I have learned to give Ryan feedback about what would mean the most to me, such as having conversations together in the evening without our cell phones. Little ways we have guided each other have given us the ability to communicate love in a way that we both understand. By being open to hear each other's needs and by trying our best to fulfill them, we've slowly learned how to most effectively take care of each other.

If you aren't sure what your husband's needs are, or are confused about how he communicates love, take heart! Understanding what a person's love language is can take some time. Gary Chapman made a super helpful tool called the "5 Love Languages Quiz" that you can find in the back of his book. I would recommend reading his book and taking the quiz for yourself so that you and your husband can utilize the tools he presents to enhance your communication. Also, if you, dear friend, are in the stage of communication when you and your husband are spending a couple hours at a time trying to sort things out, please don't get discouraged!

We certainly felt like those times were hard. Shoot, we even made ourselves a new couch so our butts wouldn't hurt during the long conversations that we struggled our way through. But God was good to us! Looking back over just one year, we can already see the immense improvement He has helped us to achieve. My hope is that you will persevere through the hard times and my greatest encouragement would be to keep working toward the goal of communicating love to one another.

It's just the hormones talking

Now, I have shared with you some things Ryan and I have learned about how to share feelings and care for one another's hearts. I have also talked about the lessons we have been taught regarding speaking a specific love language to each other. What I am about to address now is the very practical, somewhat humbling reality about communicating love when you, as a wife, are feeling a little less than lovely.

Raise your hand, ladies, if there are certain times of the month that you could shin-slam someone with your grocery cart, take the bag of Cheetos right out of their basket, and cut in line in front of them—and not feel one bit sorry. For those of you who didn't raise your hand, you are 55 percent more likely to commit a homicide than the general population (not actually, but acknowledging you have a problem is the first step toward healing). All joking aside, whether we want to admit it, sometimes we can have a hard time keeping our emotions under control when Aunt Flo comes for a visit. There are certainly hormonal times when I have felt the hot burn of anger in my chest over something that would normally not faze me. At those times I have a *really* hard time communicating in a respectful way with my husband, and those episodes can often lead to my hurting Ryan with my words.

One big thing we have found helps is if I can identify the root cause of why I am responding to him with uncharacteristic anger. Now, of course, it could be that I perceived something he did or said as being unloving, and in those situations we both need to work through the problem and resolve it. I will address that more in later chapters, but for now, I am just talking about when you bite your husband's head off because the sound of his chewing is bothering you. For the poor guy, behaviour like this can be pretty confusing, hurtful, and scary. I am still learning how to implement this successfully, but what we have found to be the most helpful is if I, as the wifey, can stop, take a breath, and acknowledge whether I am feeling unloved or hormonal.

If it is "just hormones" (NEVER use this terminology if you are a man), we reasonable ladies should be able to have the ovaries to say that we are feeling unusually grumpy because we have a large amount of hormones changing how our brain is reacting. As a medical professional myself, I would like to say that Shark Week is something akin to a cyclical mental health disorder, so it should be approached as such. Now, let me just stop and say that not only should men never use phrases such as "it's just hormones," they should also not disregard real feelings because you have your period. But it would take a whole other book to discuss what men in marriages should do. So, ladies, I'm just talking to you. If you feel crazy because you have raging hormones (God-given, by the way) coursing through your body, do a guy a favour and admit to not feeling very reasonable. This kind of admission isn't weakness! What you are feeling is very real, and very hard to control. But wouldn't you rather your husband think you are struggling with things going on in your body than that you are naturally a bit psychotic?

My best advice, if you are struggling with this, would be to sit down and have an open and honest conversation with your husband about strategies you could set up for when you are feeling a little psycho. In our marriage, I have agreed to verbalize when I am feeling overwhelmed or angry as a result of hormones. We have also discussed spending some time apart (like a half hour) for me to get my emotions under control before we attempt to discuss things during this time. Our strategy for conflict resolution, which I will get into in a later chapter, is normally to sit down and talk things out right away until they are resolved. When I am feeling hormonal though, we have found that this doesn't work very well. I will have an unjustified angry reaction to what Ryan is saying and will either go quiet or have an outburst of emotion. This leaves Ryan feeling like he has either (a) done something very wrong or (b) I do not respect or love him very much. I don't want either of those things for him, so we have agreed upon a game plan for certain "periods" of time during the month. However you choose to do this is up to you, but I believe it is really important to acknowledge the strong effect hormones can have on us, and to do our best to use clear and kind communication through this time.

Conclusion

There are so many ways that we can improve our communication with one another, from openly admitting out-of-control feelings to learning how to share feelings and tailoring our actions to speak love directly to our spouse's heart. Though it may feel tough or hopeless at times, we can always ask God for His help as we press toward the goal of better communication. I hope that this has encouraged you to be vulnerable about your emotions and to take the time to listen to your husband's heart. I hope that you also have some strategies that you can implement to help speak love to each other in a way that will be understood. Lastly, my greatest desire would be that you continue working at improving your communication to enjoy the security and love it can bring to your marriage.

Chapter 4:
Submission, Respect, and My Little Friend, the Ego

My jaw was set in a stubborn tilt as I stared blankly at the wall. My arms were folded across my chest and I sat, defiantly slumped into our uncomfortable orange and brown relic of a couch. A little more than a month had passed since I had changed provinces, and although I was fairly adjusted to living in my new home, I was not yet familiar with submitting to someone else's leadership.

Ryan sat beside me, elbows on his knees, hands folded in front of him, with a look on his face that made me think he was most certainly praying for strength. Though his commitment to seeking God's guidance was something I greatly admired, in that moment I was pushing for a much less holy approach to the conflict before us.

Why is he always so gentle?! I want to handle this situation my way! My frustrated brain fumed at the seeming unfairness of the situation as I stacked up evidence to support my desired plan of action.

There had been a vast amount of paperwork required in order for me to change my identification over to a new province. First my driver's licence, then my bank, then my passport, then my insurance, and finally, the last step was to have my car approved through an out-of-province inspection. We had taken my little 2008 Chevrolet Cobalt to a local mechanic and asked him to perform the inspection. When we had returned to pick it up, I had noticed that a lug nut was missing and that three of the posts they fasten to had been stripped bare, save for a few threads near the very base. Since we had picked the car up after hours, there was no one available to speak to, and the problem would have to wait until the next day. My immediate thought was a very angry one, and I decided then and there that we wouldn't pay until they had fixed what they had broken. Fast forward through my ranting about how they had ruined my car as we drove home, and there we were, locked in a stand-off, sitting in silence in the dim living room of our house.

I was a strong, independent woman. I prided myself in being stubbornly relentless and always defended myself against being taken advantage of. Therefore, when my car was returned to me in a poorer condition than I had left it, I felt it was my personal right to storm into that mechanic's shop and give him a piece of my mind. In my opinion, it would seem weak of me to allow him to walk away without taking responsibility for the damages he'd caused, and it would cause me no greater joy than to be the one to deliver that very message. Ryan, however, was of a very different opinion. He felt that, though he could see we may have been wronged, it would be a better course of action to pay the mechanic for his time and let the matter lie. With it being a small town, Ryan didn't want to make an enemy by causing a fuss, nor did he want to ruin our testimony or name. Our conflict had started when I told him I wanted to act independently of him and he had calmly replied that I couldn't. At first I was aghast that he was asking me to just drop it. His words to me had been: "We are married now, Madison. My name is your name, and as your husband, I am asking you to not pursue this any further."

Not pursuing this issue further was the last thing I had on my mind. *Why does it matter that we have the same last name? I am a grown woman; I will deal with this how I want to!* My mind spat out retorts to his statement, but I remained silent as I contemplated the decision before me. One option was to call the mechanic the next day and demand a refund. Ryan would be at work and wouldn't need to know the exact words or tone I had used to finagle a monetary return. The other option, the one that my conscience kept thrusting forward, was to submit to my husband's desires and please him and God rather than myself. That path sounded ever so right and holy, but it was the exact opposite to what I felt would be most satisfying. I thought about it a bit longer, contemplating the kind of wife I wanted to be, considering if submission was really required of me in this situation. My wedding vows sprung to my mind and I repeated one of the lines over in my head: *With the Lord's help I will learn to follow your leadership and to show you a constant, Christ-like love.* Though my stubborn mind was fighting it, in my heart I knew what I should do and what my vows, before God and my husband, required me to do. Finally breaking the silence, I spoke to Ryan,

"OK, I won't pursue this any further. I'll just go pay the bill."

~

This particular instance was just the first of many in which I had to learn to choose submission to my husband rather than my own path. The choice I made to submit in this situation was the starting point from which my convictions about submission and respect germinated and grew. Though I had come into marriage with every intention of being a godly and submissive wife, I had no idea how hard that would be until I came head to head with my husband over that issue. In the following months I not only learned so much more, but raised the standard of what I expected from myself. I decided that I wanted and needed to commit myself whole-heartedly to being submissive to Ryan. I also realized that I needed to submit, not just because it would make Ryan happy, but because it was actually something that God *required* of me. Another thing I learned was that God's desire goes beyond submission and even asks that submission be acted upon with respect. If those two things weren't enough to keep me busy, I spent some of my free periods in "School for the Wedded and Unlearned" formulating a hypothesis regarding what I now fondly refer to as Ryan's "little ego orb." This same orb has become a bit of a breakthrough in my personal understanding of what makes men and women so different from one another.

While these topics are hard to tackle and maybe even harder to learn, I am very excited to share my experiences with you because I believe that these things are some of the most important things a woman can develop in her marriage. One amazing reward for learning these truths is that God has designed the path that godly wives take to feature beautiful and rewarding gems that fulfill some of their greatest desires.

TMI: TRUTHFUL MARRIAGE INSIGHTS

My mission: submission

Society today has made submission a very taboo and non-feminist thing to pursue. I mean don't we women deserve to just burn our bras and demand respect for making our own choices? Now hold on. Before your inner feminist shouts out "YES, I DO!" consider the under-boob sweat problem you would encounter and, much more importantly, consider if that is the kind of feminism God asks of us. All joking aside, the Bible clearly shows us that the woman God desires us to be is a far cry from the demanding, self-serving form of womanhood today. What makes this so wonderful is that the role God has created for us will not only bring us joy, but it will develop in us a submission that helps our husband to fulfill his God-given role.

Picture this for a moment. Your husband is standing before God, answering for the choices your family has made and speaking about the leadership he showed in your home. When God asks him, "Why is your name scorned in your town? Why do they not associate you with Me?" your poor husband bows his head and sighs, "I tried, Father. She just . . . I couldn't stop her . . . she was so upset about the lug nuts."

Now, this particular exchange may sound crazy, but in my case, this kind of conversation could have been a real possibility if I hadn't chosen to submit to Ryan's desires. I am certainly not trying to toot my own horn, because I still struggle to choose submission on a regular basis. I am, however, trying to impress on you how very important it is that we support our husband's role of leadership by showing submission. This picture I have described is one that I played over in my head for many days following our sofa stand-off, and it's ultimately what changed my understanding of submission for the better. I realized that God has asked Ryan to lead our home, and that Ryan will actually have to stand before God and speak for the choices our household has made in a coming day. If I choose to act "independently," not showing submission or respect, I can impact what my husband has to say about our home, and I can hinder him from being the leader that God asked him to be.

While God asks for men to be leaders of their homes, not every guy is a natural-born leader. Ryan, for example, is a very gentle man who doesn't like to cause conflict and who would likely choose the route that creates the most peace. These attributes make for a very kind and understanding leader, but they could also lead to my taking advantage and assuming more of a "pants-wearing" role in our relationship. But I have learned over time that there is nothing more rewarding than using submission to help your husband develop into the leader that God designed him to be. The way that Ryan goes about things is not how I would go about them, but when I decided to choose submission I saw his confidence as a leader blossom and his spiritual life grow. I discovered that if I step back and choose to respectfully submit, I am not only fulfilling my role as a godly woman, but I'm also giving my husband the opportunity to fulfill his role as a godly man. This was just one of the many joys I've realized God wove into the fabric of His "dress" for me.

Another thing that I have seen submission do in my own life is increase how loved I feel. Now, this isn't some airy-fairy advertisement for submission—it is the honest truth. Though it is a struggle at times for me to set aside my stubborn will, I have found that, if I submit respectfully to Ryan, he feels that I am confident in his leadership and he feels respected as a man. This causes him to feel loved by me and, in turn, to pour a reciprocal love back onto me. I don't want to speak too quickly, but I seriously think I have found the magic potion to lasting love and happiness. I was going to bottle it and sell it, but it turns out that a couple thousand years ago it was already discovered and written about in the Bible. Unfortunately, over time, it seems that the concept of submission has lost its appeal, but I want to encourage you that its ability to bring you soul-deep happiness has not diminished. I still have such a long way to go, and I am so far from the meek, gentle spirit I would like to be, but through my own experience, I have become a believer in submission. While I have found that it is a choice I have to make every day, each time I choose to submit I am rewarded with the knowledge that I have done what God asks of me and that I am being respectful to my husband.

R-E-S-P-E-C-T . . . find out what it means to me

OK, I'm about to name drop another seriously good book that Ryan and I have used as a great source in our marriage. By now you likely know that none of my thoughts is original, so just sit back and learn from the accounting of my mistakes as I learned how to implement some of the tools we read about in Dr. Emerson Eggerichs' book, *Love and Respect: The Love She Most Desires, The Respect He Desperately Needs*. This book presents the idea that men feel loved by being respected and women feel loved by just being straight-up loved. It goes on to explain that if a man feels disrespected he will likely act unloving and if a woman feels unloved she will likely act disrespectful. This exchange can go on endlessly, creating what he calls the "crazy cycle," which can some-times be the cause of an unhappy marriage. It's not necessarily a novel concept, but boy does it ever explain a lot!

Ryan and I both read this book while we were dating and found it extremely helpful in how we communicated with each other. When I first came into marriage I didn't actually know what respectful behaviour or language sounded like. As I have said before, a lot of my childhood featured conflict in my parents' marriage, which I would now blame partially on the effects of an ongoing "crazy cycle" in their relationship. Because of this, I wasn't exposed to a very respectful or loving model of a marriage and came into my own unsure of how to live out these things. Thankfully, I have a very loving and awesome husband who patiently guided me into showing him more respect.

There were many times in the beginning of our marriage that I would jokingly tease Ryan about something he had said, or make a sarcastic comment that I intended all in good fun. It wasn't long, however, before I learned that this wasn't very "good fun" to him, and that it was actually quite hurtful. You see, respect is defined as "a feeling of deep admiration for someone or something elicited by their abilities, qualities, or achievements" (Google). Where I was going wrong was when I would poke fun at Ryan for saying a word incorrectly. I was making him feel like his abilities were lacking and, in turn, causing him to feel disrespected. The bell that usually went off to alert me that I had been disrespectful was when Ryan responded to me in a way that I perceived as un-loving. Rather than allow this to degrade into a "crazy cycle," we tried our best to stop and ask the other person if something we had said was disrespectful or un-loving. Usually a long conversation ensued— like the one that confirmed our need for a new couch—and the original comment was addressed and apologized for. This took a lot of time to learn and, believe me, it takes a lot of humility to hear another person say you did something wrong. With practice, though, it became easier to hear when something I was saying was disrespectful and it also became easier to discuss where we had gone wrong.

A year and a half in, and I sometimes still have to stop and ask Ryan if I've said something disrespectful. We can, however, look back and see how much we have grown in this area and it is very encouraging. There is nothing better than feeling loved in your marriage, and we are so very thankful that we have had the resources to develop loving and respectful behaviour in our home. If you haven't read the *Love and Respect* book, I would strongly recommend it and encourage you to implement the author's teaching. The best part about this source is that his ideas come from the Bible, where it says, "However, each one of you also must love his wife as he loves himself, and the wife must respect her husband" (Ephesians 5:33, NIV). Not only is God's word true and holy, it is the absolute best advice we could ever get on how to have a happy and fulfilling marriage. The fact that this is found in the Bible has also been a huge comfort to Ryan and me because we know we can ask God for His help when we find ourselves struggling to communicate. Though there is constant work needed to behave in a Christ-like way in marriage, with God's help, we have seen many rewards from our efforts to be loving and respectful to each other.

My little friend, the ego

What I learned about respectfulness in marriage soon initiated another discovery of a similar nature that dealt directly with the needs of my husband's ego. For those of you who don't know yet, I am a very visual person. My mind is often drawing up little images of things or moments that help me to better understand the topic I am contemplating. So without further ado, let me introduce you to my little friend, Ego. He is about the size of a mango, with a perfectly oval shape. He has a soft blue glow hovering around his edges, which gets brighter when he is feeling good and dimmer when he is neglected. He requires specific care to stay bright and inflated. He prefers to have someone else inflate him if he is feeling down, but if that doesn't happen, he does try to re-inflate himself. When he is over-inflated it can be ugly, but when he is under-inflated it can be even worse. I found this little Ego in my husband's pocket and was a little perturbed by his neediness in the beginning. Over time, however, I have come to understand his Ego, and would like to share with you some of the ways I have learned to care for it.

Now, you may see a man's ego a little differently than I do, but I have discovered that there are some important characteristics about an ego that can really affect the quality of your relationship. It was a couple months into our marriage when I first conjured up this humorous little depiction of something that people have been talking about and dealing with for years. I actually found the visual aid quite useful in understanding why Ryan sometimes acted the way that he did. Some days, Ryan would come home from work, complain about his workmates, describe a job he had been working on, and finish it off with a statement about the superior skills he had demonstrated. Now I am all for complimenting my incredible hubby, but I sometimes thought to myself: *Slow down, buddy. As the Bible says, "Let another praise you, and not your own mouth" (Proverbs 27:2, NKJV).* Once the initial irritation wore off, I'd get to thinking about why he felt the need to praise himself. This is when I stumbled upon my hypothesis about Ego's attributes and how it needs to be cared for.

You see, I've got this idea that Ego needs to be kept in a constant state where it is bright and inflated in order for the carrier to feel his best. While I think I originally looked at this as a chore, I have found that, with very little effort, Ryan's ego can be happily maintained and I can use this ministry to honour my husband. Something I have learned is that Ego operates on an inflation-deflation system. For example, if Ryan is criticized at work for something, his ego deflates a little. Like many other men, he really doesn't like it when his ego feels deflated, and Ryan would some-times try to inflate it himself. For whatever reason, I, like most women, really didn't like the sound of him breathing into his own ego and would inwardly roll my eyes and think: *Well, that sounded proud.* What I didn't understand at the time, though, was that it wasn't pride I was hearing but the hissing sound of a man trying to inflate his own ego back to its happy place.

The idea that the ego feels off-kilter when it is deflated and that it needs inflation from some source before the carrier feels bal-anced led me to believe that it was my job as a wife to consider the ego part of my husband and to take care of it. Since coming to that understanding, I have been able to understand statements that sound quite proud as indications that there is something wrong with Ryan's ego. This isn't a bad thing, or something to be scorned; it is simply one of the many differences between men and women. At times when I can sense his ego is feeling like a morning-after air mattress, I have learned that I should stop and ask him how he is feeling. More often than not there has been a time in the day where either I or others, have caused him to feel deflated within himself. Moments like this are perfect opportunities to give him a little bit of praise and re-affirm for him that I have full confidence in his abilities. It has been incredibly exciting and rewarding to see that when I make the effort to take care of Ryan and his ego, he feels happy and secure in my love. Though it is maybe not the most novel concept, our marriage has been blessed by the discovery of this idea and we have been able to grow in our understanding of one another because of it.

Conclusion

In this chapter, I shared a lot of my convictions and discoveries about submission, respect, and the ego. I hope that it hasn't overwhelmed you but has inspired you to seek to be the type of woman that God has asked us to be. Though submission and respect to your husband is currently an unpopular belief, I have personally experienced so many blessings in seeking to respond to Ryan with these attitudes. I have only scratched the surface in telling you the joy and fulfillment that come from following the path that God gives us—but that's OK because you can discover it for yourself! I hope that you have seen the strength and beauty in giving up your own will in order to submit to the desires of God and your husband. I hope that you have felt encouraged to find new ways to speak respectfully to and support (or inflate) your husband when he is feeling down. Most of all, I hope that this has helped you to look carefully at your marriage and determine your convictions in order to be the wife you vowed to be and the woman God wants you to be.

Chapter 5:
Dealing With Conflict

I slumped down onto the basement stairs, put my face in my hands, and cried. It was somewhere around 9 p.m., and I was tired, sad, and grumpy all in one. Ryan stood across from where I sat looking even more tired than me, yet with a caring frown furrowing his brow.

We were in my brother's basement, four days deep into a bathroom renovation that he had hired us to do. It was a dual-purpose negotiation that benefitted both parties. For me, it was a visit to my hometown to see my family, and for my brother and his wife it was a chance to get their bathroom done at a reasonable rate. The arrangement seemed perfect, and I had been looking forward to the trip for a number of weeks, but, as is often the case, what I envisioned was not exactly what happened. Our original plan was that I would spend the mornings helping Ryan and then the afternoons with my family. As the week wore on though, it became readily apparent that there was much more work to be done than one person could accomplish in the time frame we had allotted. That meant that, for the past three days, I had spent all day working with him on the bathroom, save for a few hurried meals that we ate at my parents' home.

Now we were reaching the end of the fourth day, the night slipping by, my parents no more than ten kilometres away, yet Ryan and I were still in the basement wrestling with a stubborn shower drain. I was new to the renovation world, so when we had to cut apart work we had already done in order to fit the shower into place, I felt like the project was becoming hopeless. I was stressed and overwhelmed and as the time ticked on toward 10 p.m., my emotions finally boiled over, resulting in the tears that now ran down my face and dripped onto the cement floor at my feet. Ryan, though he was feeling just as defeated as I was, came over and placed a hand on my back. With a sincere voice he said, "I'm so sorry, honey. I just don't know what to do."

I sniffled and sighed, trying to wipe away the tears that kept coming and to find the words to explain what I was feeling.

"It just feels like I can't see my family even though they are so close by right now. I know we agreed to do this bathroom together, but I didn't know what it would take, and I didn't know that it would feel so hard. And I don't know how to fix that stupid shower either!"

My last statement came out with an exasperated moan as I dropped my chin onto my fisted hands and stared bleakly at the wall. Ryan stepped closer and reached out to me, gently coaxing my hands away from my face. He held them in his own and pulled me to my feet. No sooner was I up then he wrapped me in a hug and buried his face in my neck, arms squeezing me tightly as he replied, "I just don't know how to fix it, honey. I don't know what you want me to do."

His statement came out with a sigh and I sought words to explain that the problem was just my emotions and that this situation wasn't the fixable kind. Coming up short, my shoulders lifted in a half-hearted shrug and I gave the only response I could think of. "I guess this problem just isn't about the nail."

~

Now, before you look at this book cross-eyed and think to yourself, *well, no wonder the shower wasn't working, you aren't supposed to use nails!* The type of nail I was talking about was a figurative nail, and it is an analogy that has helped Ryan and me work our way through conflict often. With time, we have learned to consider each other's perceptions, and to apologize for the part we played in the way the other person feels. It was also very important, for me especially, to learn how to forgive Ryan and to actually vocalize my forgiveness when he apologized. Another thing that has helped us through conflict was never pushing problems under the proverbial "rug," and dealing with them as soon as they happened. We both had a lot to learn when it came to communicating through conflict, but with lots of help from God, and some interesting resources, we have definitely gotten better at resolving our problems.

"It's not about the nail"

We first learned the term "It's not about the nail" through a little YouTube clip with the same name that was directed by Jason Headly. I'd recommend you watch it, as it is not only humorous, but also very insightful about the differences in how men and women communicate problems. Essentially, a man and woman are discussing their day on the couch. The woman has an actual nail sticking out of her forehead as she describes to the man that she doesn't understand why she has been having headaches, threads pulled in all of her sweaters, etc. The man keeps trying to point out that the problem is the nail in her forehead, but she finally bursts out, "It's not about the nail!"

Changing his tactic, the man decides to give her a hug and pat her back and say, "That must be really hard to be experiencing all of that."

The woman sighs and relaxes into him. Clearly feeling understood, she responds, "Yeah, it is! I'm so glad you get it."

While the whole scenario is very exaggerated and odd, this little clip pretty clearly sums up the way that most men and women solve problems. Basically, God wired men to be problem-solvers, so when a woman describes things that are causing her distress, men see these things as problems and want to fix them. Women, on the other hand, often tell others about their problems because they want to feel heard and understood and don't necessarily want the solution. This is an understanding that has often helped Ryan and me to describe our emotions and guide each other to conflict resolution.

One very important thing that we learned to do was to ask the other person what kind of solution they were seeking. For example, if I was telling Ryan about something that upset me, such as the bathroom renovation situation, he learned to ask me: "Is this about the nail?" Or, more simply: "Do you want the solution?"

If I just wanted to be heard and understood I would tell him, like I did that day in the basement, "It's not about the nail."

Communicating this way helped us to respond to each other in a way that diffused, rather than ignited, conflict.

Something that I learned, when trying to communicate about problems, was that Ryan couldn't read my mind. I know, it's shocking, really, that despite scientist's claims of evolution, men still can't read women's minds. You would think that this kind of upgrade would really increase male survival rates. In any case, the fact still remains that men, no matter how understanding and connected they are, can't know what you are thinking.

Thankfully, when God was creating us, He crafted the perfect solution. *Talking!* Yup, simple as it seems, I really had to learn how to communicate my needs to Ryan in order to get the kind of response I was looking for. At the same time, he learned to ask me what kind of response I needed rather than just provide me with a solution—though I know he sometimes desperately wanted to! It took some time to get good at, but with practice, we learned how to voice our needs in a conversation and respond to each other in a way that showed care.

In the same way that Ryan was careful to ask me what kind of response I was looking for, I had to be careful not to stifle his God-given desire to fix problems. It became apparent, a little after stumbling across this video, that while a wife may just want her husband to listen, a man has a need to protect and care for his wife.

I learned that the reason Ryan would want to immediately solve my problem was because God had hard-wired him to care for me that way. Though it took some effort to achieve, with time, we found a balance that met both of our needs and helped us to better communicate.

He would take the time to listen to my problems, and offer the desired, "That's too bad" and "Aww that must be hard." This made me feel cared for and understood and, because of it, I felt loved and would ask him what he thought I could do to fix the problem. He then felt respected and had the ability to fulfill his role of leadership in our home. Once it had come full circle, I felt loved, he felt respected, and we both felt like we had experienced a communication win!

Three sides

You know that saying, "There are three sides to every story—your side, my side, and what actually happened"? Well, through the first year of marriage, I have come to the conclusion that there certainly *are* three sides to every story, and each is 100 percent right. Now I know that you are likely thinking that every side being right just isn't possible, but hear me out. For the visual learners like me, imagine you are driving in a car on the highway with your husband. You are both looking out the window taking in the scenery, commenting on things you pass by. When you reach your destination you may find that you have seen different things. So you have your husband's version of the drive that features the seeders and combines he saw in a field, your version of the drive that features the cows and horses you saw in a corral, and the actual drive that features seeders, combines, cows, horses, cherry trees, a farm house, and some shirtless farmer mowing his lawn.

While you may not have seen the seeders, it doesn't mean they weren't there and while he may not have seen the cows, it doesn't mean that they weren't there. Neither of you was seeing things that didn't exist, but you were both only seeing part of whole picture. The important part to note is that neither your nor your husband's version was wrong—it was just incomplete and likely catered to the topics that interested you individually.

A lot of parallels from this visual can be related to conflict scenario communication. The main one that I was blessed to have learned in our marriage was that both of our perceptions are right. We may not see the conflict we are facing in the same way and our individual perception is the truth in our own mind, but there can't be two different things that are true—can there? The answer I have found is YES! Both Ryan and I can feel completely different about a topic of conflict and both be right. This means that, even when I don't think that what I said was hurtful, if Ryan perceived it as such, it *was* hurtful. It also means that when I perceived Ryan's comment to have been dismissive, it *was* dismissive. Where it is incredibly easy to go wrong is when you try to convince the other person that only *your* perception is right. This kind of response can invalidate your spouse's feelings, and we have found that it doesn't yield the desired resolution for a discussion of conflict.

When I am attempting to validate how Ryan perceived a situation, I find that my pride often gets in the way. I mean, let's face it, it is pretty darn humbling when you get told that what you said sounded very disrespectful. My immediate desire is always to defend myself, but when I do that, I overlook how my words made my husband feel, and prolong the hurt that he is experiencing. We have both learned that when we are able to put our own pride aside and listen to what the other person perceived, we are able to resolve the situation much more quickly.

It has been very important to learn how to communicate our own perception and how to apologize for our actions. Something we have tried to make a habit is saying things like, "I felt . . ." or "It seemed like to me . . ." and even, "I perceived that comment as . . ." This has proved much more effective than statements like: "You made me feel . . ." or "You said this to me . . .".

Ryan and I have found that, more often than not, when we understand the other person's perception, we are horrified at what they thought we meant. This kind of clarification has become an essential part of our conflict resolution and has aided us in clearly communicating our feelings. Through our first year, we have learned how to hear each other's perceptions, validate them, and clarify our own position when we have been misunderstood.

No matter how much we have learned and grown, there are still lots of times when we have to apologize for something we have done. When we were first married, I was surprised to find that

I hardly knew how to say the words "I forgive you." I could say I was sorry, and being the good Canadian I was, used this phrase quite frequently. However, when it came to actually vocalizing my forgiveness to Ryan, I was hesitant, and preferred to say: "It's fine."

As you may well imagine, this didn't really seem to resolve much, and it felt like I was brushing off the apology. Ryan would kindly coach me by asking me if I would please say that I forgave him. Over time, I learned the importance of this statement and have added it to the things I need to keep in mind during a conflict. While apologizing to the other person for the hurt they felt is super important, verbal forgiveness is also imperative. Being the person I am, I find I cannot say that I will forgive him unless I truly commit to forgiving him in my heart. Though this sometimes makes it harder, it also means that we properly forgive conflict before we leave the conversation and that conflict is resolved before we go to bed.

The princess and the pea

Do you ever feel like the damsel in the fairy tale about the princess and the pea? Do you ever have something, even if it is small, that just bugs you so much you can't go to sleep? That is how both Ryan and I feel if we haven't dealt with conflict before we go to bed. Something we talked about when we were dating was the importance of dealing with issues as soon as they came up. We felt that this was the best way to avoid bitterness and anger. We also like it when our relationship feels good so don't want to waste time brewing over something that could be resolved quickly by some clear communication. Early on in marriage, this meant that we usually spent a couple hours at a time discussing our way through conflict until we reached a point where both of us felt resolved about it. If you are thinking to yourself: *What? A couple of hours? Ain't nobody got time for that!* I want to encourage you that we found this extent of communication essential in order to understand each other the way we do now. Although dealing with conflict was arduous for a time, we have been able to use the communication skills we learned to deal with problems more effectively. Now we rarely have conflict that cannot be resolved within an hour or less, and we experience a lot fewer negative feelings along the way.

If you are at all like Ryan and me, you will understand what I mean when I say that sometimes the negative feelings that conflict brings can feel like a defeat. Both of us are perfectionists at heart, so we often find it feels as though we have failed when we need to deal with a problem. Conflict is like a mark on our record, and for people who like things to be perfect, it is hard not to feel like we have ruined the good times that we were previously enjoying. This kind of thinking can be hard to manage, and can be quite detrimental to how we deal with issues. One thing we have learned though is to not view a conflict as a failure, but a learning opportunity. While it is never fun to be at odds with one another, we have always found that we grow during times when we have to put extra effort into our communication. Once we have resolved our issue, we like to acknowledge that, although it may have been hard to go through, we have benefitted from working on our problem and have had a marriage win. Though in the heat of the moment it can feel anything like a win, once each of us has reached a place of resolve, we feel victorious for seeing it through and caring for each other throughout.

One thing we have found extremely important in reaching a unified resolve is asking each other about our feelings regarding the issue after a little time has passed. While we would sit and communicate for hours early on in marriage, it was still important to check in with each other after the conflict was over. Most times, we would talk at the end of the day until we could ask each other: "How do you feel about it now?" and get a positive response back. We also tried to ask a similar question the next morning just to ensure that the other person didn't have leftover feelings from the night before. For us, something isn't dealt with properly until both of us feel good about it. Though it may seem tedious and counter-productive to bring a conflict back up, it actually helped us to ensure that the other person felt completely resolved. When I would ask Ryan how he was feeling about the situation the next day, it gave him the opportunity to either reassure me that he felt resolved, or to seek further conversation to completely deal with any remaining feelings he had. In the same way, when he asked me how I felt, I had the ability to openly share any feelings that remained unresolved for me. By checking in with each other, we are able to not only solve problems, but ensure that we both still feel loved following our conflict.

Conclusion

Well, once again this has been a chapter filled with some pretty labour-intensive projects, so I hope you aren't feeling over-whelmed. I want to encourage you though that the reward you will find in establishing good conflict communication is immeasur-able. Ryan and I still have a lot to learn when it comes to this, but we have been so excited to see the growth that only one year has brought. So if you are feeling discouraged or overwhelmed keep at it! It will be well worth it in the end!

I hope that you have not only gotten some humour from, but also seen the valuable truth in being able to identify when it is or isn't about the "nail." I hope that you have also felt encouraged to see your husband's perspective and to accept responsibility for the hurt he perceived. I hope that you will work together to resolve your conflict before you go to bed and that you will continue to communicate until both of you feel loved. Most of all, I hope that you will acknowledge the victory of a resolved conflict, that you will continue to pour your efforts into your marriage, and that as you watch it grow you will smile to know that God is working to make it as amazing as it can be.

Chapter 6:
Family

My parents sat across the table from me, stiff backed, their faces taut with emotion as they barely held onto the thin veil that covered their pain. The clock on the wall behind me tick-tocked mercilessly as thick tension enveloped us and dread settled into the pit of my stomach. My siblings sat on either side of me, one aged eleven and one aged thirteen, their expressions mirroring mine as we waited with apprehension, expecting the worst.

It was the middle of March, just three months after my marriage to Ryan. I had eagerly awaited this week, as it was the first time my family was coming to visit me in my new home. Because we didn't have enough rooms to host them, my parents and two siblings had stayed at the home of a friend, just a short drive down the road. I had been up with Ryan since 5 a.m., and had sent him off to work before busying myself making preparations for a family breakfast I had planned. Once my parents woke up, they intended to get ready then drive to my home so we could spend as much of the day together as possible.

When they arrived, I could immediately tell that something was not right. I had seen all of these signs before: misty eyes, tight lips, shaky voices, and a visible rift between my parents that would have rivaled the Grand Canyon. The tension was something I was used to seeing, but had never become accustomed to. One look at my two younger siblings and I could quickly see that I wasn't the only one experiencing the grimy, sour feeling of fear sliding its arms around my insides as I waited for the coming onslaught. Though they had never seen the days when our parents were separated, they knew it was in our past, and the fear of history repeating itself was just as real for them as it was for me and my older brother. My younger siblings were about seven and nine, the same age my older brother and I had been when our parents first got back together, when their marriage once again took a turn for the worse. Since then it had been a slow spiral downward to the point where we had all approached them to ask if we should be expecting them to split again. Though we were assured that they wouldn't officially separate again, they suggested that they may live individual lives in the same house as their issues were apparently irreconcilable. The mere suggestion of an un-official split had brought back all of the overwhelming emotions I had faced as a child, and I felt no better equipped to deal with them as an adult.

Now I sat at my table, face grim, listening as my dad announced that things were not going well between him and Mom, and that he would be going home on a flight that afternoon. The learned habit of self-preservation quickly kicked in, as stone walls fell into place around my heart, blocking out as much of the pain as they could and masking the emotion on my face. I stared blankly at the wall, wondering what had caused their argument this time and aching for the pain this caused my siblings. My soul stung from the shrapnel that had hit it when the peaceful safety of my little home had been shattered. I didn't question and didn't try to reason with them. I didn't cry out like I wanted to or upbraid them for tearing apart the place of safety I had finally managed to build for myself. I simply nodded and asked when the flight left, my stone-cold attitude a desperate grasp for control as I fought to keep my emotions beneath the surface.

Before long, my dad was at the door ready to leave. Inside of me, my five-year-old self clung to her teddy bear, begging him not to go, wishing he and Mommy could figure things out. On the outside I was twenty-two, watching as my younger siblings experienced a goodbye so similar to the countless ones my brother and I had endured through our childhood as we went back and forth between our parents' homes. But, just as it was then, nothing could stop what was coming. I told my dad that I wished he could stay, saw him nod, then turn and leave my house, shutting the door behind him. Left with my two distraught siblings, I did my best to comfort them before finding an empty room and letting my walls crack apart as the emotions spilled out of my heart and I wondered, *God, how will my family ever change?*

~

This story illustrates one of the many situations in which one of our families has impacted either Ryan or me. While you may think that the influence your family has on you ends with marriage, you will soon find out that this is only true if you cut your family out of your lives. As this was something Ryan and I didn't want, we have had to learn how to navigate difficult family relationships and their effects on our marriage. Through our first year we have learned the importance of sharing our history and acknowledging how the experiences we have gone through prompt the reactions we have today. We have also learned about the selfless attitude that God wants us to love our families with, even when the dynamic of our relationship with them changes. Something else we've discovered is the importance of maintaining good relationships with your immediate family and in-laws in order to show love to your spouse. And, of course, the topic of family could not be mentioned without sharing the many things we have learned about planning for our own family and the (sometimes) dreaded discussion about tiny humans. Though we are still working on implementing the things we have learned, we are convinced that God is interested in seeing us build and maintain our relationships with our families. With His help and whole lot of prayer, I hope to share what we have discovered and encourage you throughout the maze of complicated and (often) messy family relationships.

Not quite the Brady Bunch

As I have mentioned before, I came to marriage with a lot of baggage from my childhood. Ryan and I learned very early on that a lot of my communication and behaviour had been learned in the stressful home situation I had come from. I also had a lot of defense mechanisms that would immediately engage whenever I felt scared or insecure in our marriage, which added some difficulty to learning good communication skills. What became readily apparent through this time was that I had deep pain from my past that was affecting how I responded to Ryan. In order to move forward and improve our relationship, I needed to discover what was causing me this pain and work to address the source. Thus began our process of "unpacking" the baggage of my past and uncovering the deeply buried memories that still plagued my heart. Ryan's favourite line would be, "I've got a theory," I would say, "OK, Dr. Phil, lay it on me." From there, he would kindly communicate how a behaviour I now had was likely tied to a hurt from the past. Then we would go digging. Ryan would hold me quietly as I tried to identify something in my past that was dictating the way I was now acting. Usually it didn't take long before I unearthed a painful memory that I could identify as the cause of the response I was exhibiting. Once I addressed the pain in my past, I would be able to recognize how it had influenced my actions or reactions, and could then objectively see ways that I needed to change. Through our first year of marriage, we have gone digging for memories many a time. Each time, we have been able to identify the source of my pain and address it from a perspective that has helped me to heal.

In our marriage, I have experienced a lot of situations where I have had to uncover my past in order to heal. For example, during the winter Ryan and I would watch a lot of TV during the weekend when he was off work. Though we were careful about what we watched and though we were spending time together, I would always end the week feeling distraught and upset. When he would ask me what was wrong, I could only shrug my shoulders, unable to identify what had given me those feelings. It wasn't until we did some digging that I realized they were connected to something in my childhood. As children, when we would stay with my dad, my brother and I would watch a lot of TV. In the moment, I would think that it was fun, but as the weekend progressed, I would feel distraught and sad that I would soon have to say goodbye to my dad. I realized, at that point in my childhood, I had connected the activity of watching TV with feelings of sadness and regret. Although the situation was very different when Ryan and I were watching TV, I still ended up with the same feelings because the activity aroused emotions that were rooted in my childhood experience. After realizing this, I was able to address these emotions in myself when they arose and rationalize within myself that the situation was vastly different. With time, and some positive inner dialogue, I was able to break the connection between this activity and my emotions and heal from the pain this memory caused me.

Some memories from my childhood still bring me a lot of pain, but with God's help, I have been able to heal and have forgiven those involved in my past. If this is something you are struggling with, let me encourage you to keep pressing on. I know that revisiting some memories is very difficult, but I also know that God has been by my side every time I have had to walk through the dark paths of my past. In the same way that He was with me, I know that He will be with you! Though you may need your husband to hold you and some tissues nearby, complete and perfect healing can happen when you address the pain of your past. With a healed and refreshed heart, God will be able to shape and mould you into the wife and daughter that He desires you to be.

Despite the many emotions that our past or present experiences with family can bring up, it is still incredibly important to maintain relationships with the clan God has given you. While Ryan wanted me to honour my family bond, he found it hard to see the pain they caused me and struggled not to push them away to protect me. Initially, it confused him that I could feel so hurt by them and yet love them and want to call them on a regular basis. With time, he has understood my need for family closeness, and has also helped me to create the boundaries I need to protect myself from their turmoil. In the same way, I have attempted to help Ryan maintain the relationship he has with his family. At times, this can be difficult for both of us because we want to protect each other from the pain that family can unknowingly inflict. What we have learned, however, is that God expects us to show Christ-like love to not only one another but our families. Learning how to implement this has had its challenges, but we both acknowledged that

God has asked us to "honour our father and mother" (Ephesians 6:2, NIV). The practical application of this in our lives has been working cheerfully for our families and putting time into maintaining our relationships with them. It has also meant sacrificing our own emotional comfort in order to listen to their needs and make their desires an important factor in some of our decisions. This has not been a walk in the park and, believe me, I'm no descendant of Mother Teresa. But by understanding what God desires for us, we have been able to accept this as a responsibility and do our very best to achieve what is required of us.

At a time when we were finding this really difficult, God showed us a passage in Philippians 2:7-8: "Rather, He made himself nothing by taking the very nature of a servant, being made in human likeness. And being found in appearance as a man, He humbled himself by becoming obedient to death—even death on a cross" (NIV). We felt as though we had done enough for our families and were ready to separate ourselves from them and the pain they caused. Then God showed us what He was willing to do for us, and our whole perspective changed. Now, I was still the flawed human that I am today, and remarked that it sure was a "bummer" that God expected such a holy response out of us. Despite my sarcastic quip, we were both very humbled by the sacrifice God made for us, and marveled that He could show such love to people who treated Him with such disdain. This verse has inspired us, despite the difficulty of relationships, to do our very best to show this kind of sacrificial love to the people that make up our family.

Now, I have most definitely not mastered the art of sacrificial love, and often have a less-than-stellar attitude about aiming to be Christ-like. If you feel the same way then know you are not alone! It has felt frustrating, it has felt hard, and it has sometimes felt like the least rewarding thing I could do (I am a person who thinks that administering a throat-punch would feel quite rewarding at times). Despite these very human feelings, I know that doing what God has asked of me will bring its own reward and that I have the opportunity to use this struggle to become more like Him. No matter how hard it gets, no matter how much pain your family brings, and no matter how difficult it is to love your in-laws, I encourage you to keep trying to show the love of Christ to them. From my own experience, I can testify that it will help you be more like Christ, strengthen your bond with your family, and give you an opportunity to show love to your spouse.

In-laws and Outlaws

Someone told us once that the difference between in-laws and outlaws was that one was "wanted." Not wanting this to be true of our families, Ryan and I have tried our best to establish relationships with our in-laws and show the same Christ-like love to them that we do to our blood relatives. Because I moved to the province where Ryan and his family live, this has been something I have had the most opportunity to work on. I can tell you that there have been tricky situations and that I have had to show a lot of grace and forgiveness. I can tell you that caring for my husband's family hasn't always produced positive results and we are still working on our relationship with them. Despite all of that, I can also happily tell you that all of this effort *has* been something I've used to show my husband love and has brought us closer as a couple.

Now, for some of you who have known your husbands' families for a long time, the transition from acquaintances to in-laws may not have been too difficult. For Ryan and me, our eight-month relationship hardly gave us enough time to get to know each other, never mind our respective parents. This meant that when I moved out to Manitoba, I was quickly surrounded by his family, about whom I knew very little. It took time and work to get to know them, and there were times when I struggled with this as there were many differences in how we viewed things. What I learned, though, was that the work I was putting into building a connection with Ryan's family was actually working to build a connection between Ryan and me. It was important to him that I tried to establish bonds with his parents and the effort I was putting in really made him feel loved.

Before you get to thinking that it was all just one big tea party, you should know that even though I had the best intentions, there were still lots of times when becoming friends with my husband's family was a struggle. On a few occasions, Ryan had to listen to me rant about my feelings after an encounter with a relative that had left me feeling hurt or misunderstood. This was often hard for him, but he understood that, at the end of the day I was still committed to loving his family as a service to him. Though this didn't often play out as the perfect scenario I intended it to be, with time, I have become closer to his family and gained an understanding of them that helps me to show them love.

If you have just recently gotten married and are wondering what to do about your in-laws, here are some things I have learned. First, every single family is different. For example, in my home, we were raised to celebrate Christmas, birthdays, and just about any holiday in which you could put out tacky decor and gather around food. In Ryan's home, while they still celebrate Christmas and birthdays, far less emphasis is placed on these holidays and the fanfare is either minimal or non-existent. This took a bit of getting used to for me and it felt odd to pass someone's birthday without having a party for them or grabbing them by the ankles and wrists and flinging them in the air once for every year they had been alive (traditions, people!). Thankfully, my husband is a very accommodating man, and has happily incorporated many of these holidays and traditions into our own home. What I learned from this was that every family has different traditions and that it is important discover what your in-laws' traditions are and accept them for who they are. While my in-laws may never make my traditions their own, Ryan and I can establish our home to meet our needs and enjoy the different views each of our families has.

The second thing I learned is that every family communicates differently. In my family, there is a lot of joking and sarcasm. In Ryan's family, this isn't quite as prevalent, and they are careful to not say rude things to one another. This was fairly easy to adapt to, since I had been learning how to speak with words of affirmation to Ryan, but there were still times when I had to stop myself from saying a joking comment that would have been perceived as rude. My husband was also raised, until about the age of twelve, as a conservative Mennonite, and I soon learned that there were a lot of subjects that were culturally taboo. Being the blunt person I am, I have spent a fair bit of time at their table with a red face and my hand over my mouth.

One instance that was particularly humorous was a dinner at Ryan's grandparents' house. Ryan's aunt was asking a question about a butt joint in relation to a project that was being built on the property. It was explained to her that the term referred to two pieces of wood that butted up against one another at a right angle. Without thinking about my audience or the lack of cultural appropriateness, I blurted out, "Well, that is very interesting, but what about crack-fill?"

Though this still strikes me as funny, I am learning to think through my words before they leave my mouth in an effort to show respect to his family. I may be at an elementary level in this particular subject, but I am working to improve the way I communicate with them, and will hopefully refrain from creating too many embarrassing situations in the future.

The last thing I have learned is one of the biggest things I have discovered in relation to in-laws. Rather than it being something that pertains directly to me, however, it is something that mostly affects my husband. After getting married, Ryan was very cognizant of his God-given responsibility to care for me first, *then* for his family. In the beginning, I was finding it hard to establish relationships with my in-laws, and would often turn to my husband for support in difficult situations. Because of this, Ryan found it hard to maintain his relationship with his family because of the responsibility he felt to protect me. Over time, I have learned that, although I can confide my in-law troubles with him, I need to reassure him that my goal is always for us to establish and maintain a good relationship with his family. Though I can be frustrated for a time, I have learned that I need to sum up disgruntled commentary with a statement about my desire to love his family. He can then be confident that even if a situation between me and his family is frustrating, I will continue to try to reach out in love, though I may need his support along the way. This takes a lot of pressure and worry off him and gives him the ability to work on his own relationship with his family without feeling the need to intervene between them and me. All of the things we have learned have helped Ryan and me to grow closer to one another and establish bonds with each other's families. Though it is not always easy, working on our relationships with our family members is something that is God-honouring, rewarding, and loving to our spouse.

Tiny Humans

So far, we have discussed difficult family relationships, how our pasts affect our presents, and loving our spouse through loving their family. No discussion about family could be complete, however, without sharing what we have learned in relation to the topic of babies (or, as Ryan likes to refer to them, tiny humans).

In the beginning of our relationship, I was certain that Ryan's interest in me would be a passing fad, and in order to protect myself, I subconsciously did everything I could to scare him off before my heart got attached. In one conversation early on, I took it upon myself to inform him that I had always wanted twenty-four kids. While this is not a method I would recommend you implement, to my surprise and pleasure, this tactic didn't work to scare Ryan off. It did, however, coin the term "tiny humans," as Ryan couldn't bring himself to discuss the taboo topic of *babies* with me, his girlfriend of only two months.

Though this was hardly an advisable way to broach the subject with my then-boyfriend, over time, we have been able to establish better communication skills when discussing this topic. Through subsequent conversations, the number of children I want to have has been considerably decreased, and Ryan and I have reached a place where we can talk comfortably about starting our own family in the future.

Even once we were married, the topic of babies was a hard one to broach. For me, it was something I had thought about since I was a child. I had played house, pretended to be a mom to my dolls, and dreamed of one day growing up and having babies of my own. In my mind, it was the pinnacle of female success! For Ryan, on the other hand, it was a thought that was very new and very frightening. Having children had been an option to him, and one that he hadn't quite decided on. Whenever the topic arose, I would talk about having a baby with a dreamy look in my eyes and express a longing for that stage of life. Ryan would listen to this for a few moments, then try to change the topic or make the non-committal response of, "One day." Initially this was extremely hard for me, and I felt like he was crushing my hopes of ever becoming a mother. With time, however, I have learned that this was his way of communicating that he wasn't ready yet. Though this may not be the case for everyone, if it is similar to your situation, take heart! I have learned that, for many new husbands, the dream of being a father is brand new, and hasn't taken root in their heart like it has for many wives. We discovered that I could help this dream to take root by encouraging and affirming the qualities I saw in him that would make a great father. This helped him to gain confidence and open his heart up to the possibility of making some "tiny humans" of our own. The most helpful thing we have done, in order to align our dreams and make plans for our future, is pray. By taking this topic to God, Ryan now has peace about one day having children, and I have peace about waiting for God's timing. Though at times this was a scary topic to address, by asking God to guide our lives, we placed our trust in Him and can look forward to the future that He planned for us.

Another thing that we have prayed about is establishing our convictions and discussing our goals for parenting the children God may one day give us. While you may think that this is putting the cart before the proverbial horse, we have learned that it is very helpful to talk about these things before any children are actually in our lives. Earlier in this chapter I discussed some of the differences between Ryan's family and my family. As you can imagine, the difference in our upbringing has been something that we have considered in relation to our own plans for parenting. Though there are things that both of our parents have done that we don't wish to repeat, there are also many valuable lessons and convictions that they have taught us. Over the course of the past year, we have learned the value of discussing family situations in our day-to-day lives and considering the course of action we would want to take with our own children. This has helped us to understand each other's viewpoints, and establish a general plan for our home. While we are light years away from having it all figured out, with God's help, we will be somewhat prepared when He entrusts a "tiny human" to our care.

Conclusion

In this chapter, I shared a lot about my personal history with my family and the things I have learned along the way about making these relationships work. If you are experiencing some of the difficulty I described, I hope I have encouraged you to know that you are not alone. There are days when you may feel like giving up, but hang in there! It may not all come together right away, but with work, it is entirely possible to show love to both your family and your husband's family. I hope that what I have shared will persuade you to address the areas of pain in your past that may be affecting your present actions and that you will seek God's help to heal. I hope that you will feel inspired to talk about your future together and pray for God's guidance in making a plan for your own little family. Most of all, I hope that you will do your very best to follow God's call to unconditional love and seek to establish and maintain your marriage, family, and in-law relationships.

Chapter 7:
Growing Together

It was dawn and the sunlight was streaming through the windows into our little kitchen. I was shuffling around in a sleepy haze, putting together Ryan's lunch while taking out the ingredients I would need to make him breakfast. Down the hall, I could hear the sounds of him brushing his teeth and getting ready for his day at work. I smiled to myself, wondering which of his plaid shirts my country-loving husband would be wearing today. As if on cue, I heard Ryan's footsteps behind me and felt his arms wrap around my waist as he buried his face into my neck for a kiss.

This morning routine was one I had become oh-so familiar with over the past year and a half and I wouldn't do anything to change it. I knew that in a few moments, Ryan would pull out his phone and begin reading to us from the Bible. While he read, I would prepare us some breakfast then we would sit down together and eat while we discussed what we had read or what lay before us in the day.

The reading that day was in the first epistle of John, chapter four. As Ryan read out the familiar words of verse eighteen, I smiled. "There is no fear in love; but perfect love casts out fear, because fear involves torment. But he who fears has been made perfect in love" (NKJV). There had been many days in our early marriage where fear seemed to overwhelm me, but now, as I looked back, I could see that the Christ-like love that Ryan had shown me had helped to conquer all of those fears. What was even more was that the love Ryan showed me not only cast out my fears, but gave me a much better understanding of the character of God and His unconditional love toward us. Hearing that passage read reminded me of how far we had come, and how delighted I was to live in a marriage that was free from fear, where my husband and I both felt perfectly in love. In that moment, I closed my eyes and sent up a quick prayer of thanks for the unbelievable blessings that God had brought into my life.

It wasn't long before breakfast was on the table and we both tucked into plates of egg scrambler and homemade tortillas. We discussed the news and the weather, commenting intermittently on the early-morning antics of our bunnies in their backyard cage as we looked out the kitchen window. When breakfast was done,, we moved our plates aside, joined hands, and bowed our heads in prayer.

For the next few minutes, we took turns speaking to our heavenly Father. We brought Him our burdens for our friends, prayed for the preservation of our families, thanked Him for each other, and asked Him about our future. With our heads bowed and our hands intertwined, my heart sent up a silent prayer to God.

"Thank you, God, for all that you have given me. Thank you for bringing Ryan into my life—he is such an amazing husband and friend. Thank you for teaching me how to be respectful, and for helping us whenever problems arise. I didn't know what unconditional love was before, but you used Ryan to teach me that and I'm so grateful. Help me to be a loving wife. Help me to fulfill my vows every day. And, God, please help me to love Ryan the way that you have asked me to love Him."

~

Do you know how amazing it feels to be loved *unconditionally*?! Do you know how freeing it is to have all of your fears erased by perfect love? Through our early marriage, we had lots of ups and downs, but this morning as we went through our usual routine, I couldn't help but stop for a quiet prayer of thanks to God. We have been married for over a year and a half now, and still nothing is more precious to me than the lessons I have learned about love's power over fear and the way love can be used to free your spouse. Also, nothing has been more impactful on our marriage than realizing what God expects from us as seen in the Bible and enjoying the blessings that come with following His perfect plan. These two things have become the foundation of the peace and love we now experience in our marriage and my desire is to share them with you in the last few pages of this book.

Fear and Love

Long before we ever knew each other, God was preparing Ryan for our marriage in a very special way. As excited as I was about the thought of being loved, when God brought me to Ryan, I was absolutely terrified about being married. I hadn't always been so afraid, but after watching my parents struggle with their marriage for years, I promised myself that I wouldn't be married if I couldn't do it any better. At one point, I even told Ryan that I was unwilling to marry him if we weren't certain that we would have a good marriage. While I have come to learn that it is only through the power that God gives us that we are able to have a good marriage, I have also discovered that we only have freedom to enjoy our marriage when we are free of fear. Thankfully, God had already revealed this truth to my husband, and Ryan was then able to share it with me in the early months of our marriage.

Ryan had first seen the truth about love's power to overcome fear a few years before we started a relationship. After seeing his first glimpse of this amazing truth, he began to dig deeper and develop a better understanding of the subject. He shared the thoughts that he compiled on the subject with me early in our relationship through a text message that contained the following revelations:

What was the first consequence of sin? FEAR.

Read Genesis 3:10, "So he said, I heard your voice in the garden and I was afraid because I was naked and I hid myself"(NKJV). This passage brings out one of the first reaction of fear: fleeing or trying to escape. The word fear can actually be made into an acronym that reads as F.E.A.R.: forget everything and run. But fear also does more than make us run—it makes us slaves, as well. Hebrews 2:14 describes this well when it says, "In as much then as the children have partaken of flesh and blood, He Himself likewise shared in the same, that through death He might destroy him who had the power of death, that is, the devil, and release those who through fear of death were all their lifetime subject to bondage"(NKJV). This verse tells us that fear enslaves us and it makes us do things to attempt to avoid the outcome of what we are afraid of.

If you look around, there are entire industries that are created to help us avoid our fears. The cosmetic industry is there because many people fear that they aren't beautiful, anti-aging treatments are available because people are afraid of growing old, anti-anxiety pills because people are afraid of being scared, and alcohol because people are afraid of remembering. People serve these things by working for them and paying for them, time and time again, because they are enslaved by fear.

This makes fear one of the devil's great tools as it distracts us from serving God while we are sitting in the corner chewing our fingernails or looking for monsters under our bed. Instead, we should be on our knees talking to God because He doesn't want us to be afraid.

1 John 4:18 says, "There is no fear in love; but perfect love casts out fear, because fear involves torment. But he who fears has not been made perfect in love"(NKJV). The kind of perfect love that we need can only come from one source—God!

God even further shows His understanding and provision for human fear in 2 Timothy 1:7, where it says, "For God has not given us a spirit of fear, but

*of power and of love and of a sound mind" (NKJV).
This verse shows us the three biggest fears that
people have: not being in control, not being loved,
and not having a sound mind. Amazingly, though,
God's love conquers all fear because it is based on
the strongest power, love, and mind in the universe:
His own!*

*Now, obviously there are many examples in the
Bible of Christ's love, but without a doubt, the
greatest example of love is shown at the cross. On
the cross, Christ selflessly gave His life so that we
could live a life free of fear and full of His bounti-
ful and rich love. In Matthew 10:28, it says, "And
do not fear those who kill the body but cannot kill
the soul. But rather fear Him who is able to destroy
both soul and body in hell" (NKJV). Faith and fear
both demand that you believe in something you
cannot see; the choice is yours. You can remain in
fear of the things that the world has done or may do
to you, or you can put your faith in God's perfect
love that frees us from the bondage of fear and lets
us serve Him. (Ryan Penner)*

What God had instilled in Ryan was that fear was not supposed
to rule a Christian's life and that His incredible and powerful love
was the only way to truly conquer the fears we have. This understanding is something that has directed and enhanced our marriage as we have both been able to be open about our fears and
take them to God so His love could wash them away. We have also
learned that a Christ-like love (unconditional, sacrificial, patient,

and sustaining) is the only way that an individual can help their spouse overcome fear.

The acronym that Ryan came up with (F.E.A.R.: forget every-thing and run) perfectly described my response when I was feeling afraid at the beginning of our marriage. You remember that time I told my husband of two weeks I wanted to go home? Since then, I cannot tell you how many times Ryan has held me and listened to my fears. Rather than try to argue with my fears or rationalize a plan to overcome them, he has simply and quietly loved me until my fears slipped away in the wake of his unconditional affection. From the time I told him I wanted to leave to the time my parents came and upset my perfect world, Ryan has always held fast to his belief that loving me like Christ loves me will be the true remedy to my fears. And you know what? It has worked every single time.

Loving each other like Christ loves us isn't always easy, and we are far from attaining the perfection that He displays, but I want to encourage you to keep trying. When I first began my marriage to Ryan I was completely riddled with fears. I was afraid of failing at marriage, afraid of being unloved, afraid of being unhappy, afraid of anger, and afraid of disappointing my husband. Now, though, I can look back and see where God and my husband have helped me to let go of every one of those fears. With fearless freedom, I am able to love my husband with reckless abandon and feel a security and safety in our marriage that I have never felt before. If you are still facing many fears, don't give up! It may take time, but allowing God's love to remove all of your fear will release you to enjoy the beauty of the marriage He has placed you in. Also, learning to love each other like Christ loves us just gets us one step closer to fulfilling His design for a perfectly wonderful marriage.

Married to Jesus

Now, before you freak out and think to yourself, *Uh, lady, read your Bible! Jesus wasn't married*, allow your imagination to run wild for a second and picture what it would actually be like to be married to Jesus. He was perfect, He was eternally loving, He was patient, and He thought we were worth *dying* for. Sounds like a pretty AMAZING husband, right?!

While our earthly spouses are human and cannot be all of those things, did you know that we are called to love and respect them just like we would Jesus, if He was our husband? Ryan and I have discovered some insight on this topic in the book of Ephesians, chapter five, where Paul says, "Wives, submit to your own husbands, as to the Lord. For the husband is head of the wife, as also Christ is head of the church; and He is the Savior of the body. Therefore, just as the church is subject to Christ, so let the wives be to their own husbands in everything. Husbands, love your wives, just as Christ also loved the church and gave Himself for her, that He might sanctify and cleanse her with the washing of water by the word, that He might present her to Himself a glorious church, not having spot or wrinkle or any such thing, but that she should be holy and without blemish. So husbands ought to love their own wives as their own bodies; he who loves his wife loves himself. For no one ever hated his own flesh, but nourishes and cherishes it, just as the Lord does the church. For we are members of His body, of His flesh and of His bones. For this reason a man shall leave his father and mother and be joined to his wife, and the two shall become one flesh. This is a great mystery, but I speak concerning Christ and the church. Nevertheless, let each one of you in particular so love his own wife as himself, and let the wife see that she respects her husband" (verses 22-33, NKJV).

Reading this passage, we learned that Ryan's role falls under what Christ would do, and my role falls under what the church would do. Wanting to learn exactly what that meant for me, I asked myself what the role of the church was in the Christ/church relationship described. I came to find that the church is supposed to be a testimony to Christ's love. It is supposed to worship Christ, and it is supposed to try to help others establish their own relationship with Christ. Understanding this opened up my eyes to the immense intricacy in God's plan for marriage and the correlations that could be drawn between our spiritual relationship with Christ and our earthly relationship with our spouse.

First of all, I was challenged by the fact that the Church needed to be a testimony to Christ's love. If Ryan is fulfilling the role of Christ in our marriage, I am called to respond to him like the church does to Christ. So with that knowledge, I sought to understand what I needed to do to be a testimony to Ryan in our marriage. I have come to find that I can do this by submitting to him and being respectful of his role as leader in our home. Like I learned in the incident with the lug nuts on my car, I need to carry our name with the dignity and grace that my husband has established for us.

Secondly, I discovered that I needed to, in some sense, worship Ryan. While this obviously is not indented to place him on the same level as Christ, it is an attitude of reverence and respect that can be used to show him my delight in him. This can be acted on in many ways, but as I have mentioned before, I have learned that the way I speak about Ryan and the attitude with which I do things for him communicate my admiration to him.

The third thing I realized is that I need to seek to help others establish their own relationship with their "Christ." Though I know that there is only one Christ and Saviour, the picture of a husband as Christ is something that each of us can take for ourselves. Therefore, I need to find ways to encourage those around me to establish and strengthen their relationships with their spouses. This discovery brought me to the place I am this very moment—finishing a book about the things we have learned in marriage with the hope that they may impact even one couple on their marital journey.

Conclusion

Though I feel completely inadequate to pass on marriage advice or counsel, we are extremely passionate about marriage, and want nothing more than to see marriages succeed. Of all the pictures in the Bible, marriage is the one thing that can truly mimic Christ's love for the church, which is a message that people in our world *need* to hear and see. I have seen so many marriages fail, so many marriages be reduced to painful monotony, and so many marriages negatively impact the lives of Christians. But Christ wants so much more for us!

Every day is a new lesson and we still have so many more things to learn, but Ryan and I are dedicated to working to make our marriage the best it can be for the rest of our lives. I hope that this book has been an encouragement to you. I hope that you have felt understood and empowered to continue striving. And, most of all, I hope that you will put your whole energy, effort, and commitment into working everyday to grow your marriage into what God designed it to be.

Notes

Chapter 2: Intimacy

1. *Iron Man 2*. (2010). [DVD] Directed by J. Favreau. United States: Marvel Studios, Fairview Entertainment.
2. Wright, C. (1970). *Express Yourself*. [Radio] United States: Warner Bros.

Chapter 3: Communication

1. Chapman, G. (2015). The 5 Love Languages. United States: Moody Publishers.

Chapter 4: Submission, Respect, and my little friend Ego

1. Eggerichs, D. (2004). *Love and Respect: The Love She Most Desires; The Respect He Desperately Needs*. 1st ed. United States: Integrity Publishers.

Chapter 5: Dealing with Conflict

1. Headley, J. (2013). *It's Not About The Nail*. [online] YouTube. Available at: https://www.youtube.com/watch?v=-4EDhdAHrOg [Accessed 5 Jul. 2019].
2. Christian Andersen, H. (1835). *The Princess and the Pea*. Copenhagen: C. A. Rietzel.

Chapter 7: Growing Together

1. A text message containing all original thoughts and ideas from Ryan Penner was used with his permission.

Printed in Canada